BROWNIES
FOR BREAKFAST

A COOKBOOK FOR DIABETICS
AND THE PEOPLE WHO LOVE THEM

Simple. Sugar-free. Vegan-friendly.
Whole food, plant-based eating that's good for everybody.

BY LYNNE PARMITER BOWMAN

for Helen

Table of Contents

Welcome to Old Dog Farm. Come on in.

Pull up a chair.

Introduction

Why should you take cooking tips or dietary advice from me, a crabby wannabe cowgirl who will never see 70 again, doesn't own a restaurant, isn't a TV star, doesn't have a medical degree, and doesn't particularly like to cook?

Excellent question. I asked myself the same thing.

Here's why. I was diagnosed with type 2 diabetes more than thirty years ago, and my numbers are still barely into diabetic range. The only medication I take is a minimal dose of metformin (Glucophage) once a day. I can walk uphill for miles. I can hold a plank for...well, let's just say I can hold a plank. My eyes are okay. My fingers are a little beat-up but still functional. And, hey, I still clean up pretty well.

The difference between me and so many other diabetics is that I knew early in my life that type 2 diabetes was probably in my future. My dad was diabetic. His mother was diabetic. So when I gained 60 pounds with my first pregnancy and was delivered via c-section of a nearly 10-pound baby boy, it wasn't a big surprise to be told afterward that I apparently had undiagnosed gestational diabetes, and I should expect to develop full-blown type 2 diabetes when I turned 40 or so.

Here I am, just slightly retouched, in my very own kitchen at Old Dog Farm. Enter at your own whisk!

3

Two more babies and a dozen years later, I asked to be tested for diabetes, which, apparently, hardly anybody ever asked to do. People get tested when they suspect, or their doctor suspects, that they're in trouble. Most people don't want to think about it if they don't have to. My reason for wanting to be on top of it was that my mother had died when she was in her mid-forties, from chronic kidney disease over which she had no control. She had grown weaker and sicker over a period of years, and died just after I left for college. As a result, I have deep, personal knowledge of what chronic illness does to a family, emotionally and financially.

When I became a single mom and sole support of three kids who were just two, three, and four, I was determined not to leave them, or be unable to care for them, if it was within my power to keep breathing and stay upright and functional. I never wanted my little ones to wonder, as I had, if I would still be there for them when school got out in the afternoon, or when they woke up in the morning.

Casa Chiquita at Old Dog Farm.

4

So I kept asking until someone agreed to order a HgA1c test. Sure enough, I was edging over the "normal" line into "uh-oh" territory. Bit by bit, by trial and error, I got better about eating well and exercising. I also realized as I tried to bumble my way through, that there wasn't a lot of good help out there. I was on my own.

After working at this since about 1986, I offer myself as living proof that you can cook, eat, and walk your way out of type 2 diabetes, or at least, most of the ill effects of it. That's what I want for you, and the people who love you.

In fact, I tried to weasel out of writing this book.
I was just fine being an at-home grandma, doing community work, hideously overdressing for every occasion, and going braless the rest of the time. I was kinda, sorta, working on a sugar-free recipe book. Then in one epic hour-or-so-long phone conversation with my daughter, Brynja, a nurse practitioner, she told me—again—how few folks understand what a type 2 diabetic "diet" should look like, or would follow it if they knew what it was. What usually happens when someone is newly diagnosed with type 2 diabetes, according to Brynja, is that they leave their doctor's office with little or no idea what to do about food.

But then, the clincher. She told me about an afternoon spent getting a new patient at the hospital settled in. "Ma, he's a vet. About your age. Out-of-control diabetic. He's in pain, miserable, and about to lose his legs. I told him about you, about how you were working on this book to help people beat this disease with food. With brownies! He got tears in his eyes, reached his arms out to me, and begged me to 'tell her to finish that book. Do that book, for me. I needed that book. Please tell her.'"

So, she told me. A couple of years and something of a journey later, here's that book.

It's a personal book, from me to you. It's not academic or medical. It's as close as I can come to sitting down at the kitchen table with you, one eyebrow raised in that "let's fix this" grandma way, and talking you into doing the things you need to do right now to get healthier and stay healthy as long as you can.

Eat Yourself Happy

If you've been diagnosed with type 2 diabetes, or love somebody who has, this book is for you. You folks with fatty liver disease, acid reflux, high blood pressure, excess weight, skin problems, allergies? It's for you, too. The prescription is the same. Then there's your spirit, which may be sagging, along with your upper arms. And howbout family drama? Climate change. Health care. Income inequality. Pollution of all kinds. Bees, dirt, water...problems!

No worries. Even though it all seems so huge, so insurmountable, you can do something about a lot of it right here, right now. You can improve your health, lift your spirits, help stop plastic pollution, save the earth, give your kids a better start in life...let's see, are we leaving anything out? Oh, improve your relationships, live longer...

And did we mention save a boatload of money? That should be enough to make you happier, right there.

All this you get by fixing your food yourself, from real, whole foods.

Mostly plants.

Two surefire mood lifters: Hedy the Mutt and big ripe blackberries.

We human beings are meant to feed each other.

It's an act of love and a sacrament. It's sustenance, survival, and culture. Not that other creatures don't feed each other; they do. But without that combination of opposable thumbs and a frontal cortex specially adapted for marketing, the other non-human creatures of the earth were never able to abandon their natural feeding habits. It is we humans who moved away from fishing, hunting, and foraging, into supermarket aisles full of Doritos and Dr. Pepper. What has been lost for us as a result is the habit of sitting down with friends and family to eat actual food, prepared by and with an actual human of our acquaintance, at an actual table.

Is cooking at home really better? In a word, yes, if you can possibly do it. Putting home-cooked food on the table is good for you, good for your health, good for your soul, if you have one, and for your family, if you have one. If you don't have a family, cooking is a good way to get one. Send a great fragrance wafting down the hall...that fresh pesto you're grinding, soup, maybe a cake...leave the door ajar, and the next thing you know, someone will have stuck their snoot in. It's as old as time.

When you eat food you haven't prepared yourself, you have no idea what's in it. Even if you read the labels, you still don't know. Eating takeout or in restaurants? You don't know what the blazes is in that food. *If you're diabetic, or don't want to be, you need to know what's in everything you eat.* Not suggesting you obsess about it, but make it a habit to know. At first, until it becomes a habit, go ahead and obsess about it.

Preparing your own food, then sitting down to an actual table and eating it, gives you knowledge of two things. First, you know what's in that food. Second, you have at least an inkling of what's going on in the minds of the people you're sharing the meal with.

And, yes, that will mean thinking things up to eat, then sourcing the ingredients, then putting the ingredients together, then setting the table, and finally, cleaning up. But the rewards are worth it.

A huge amount of what's wrong with the world, or your part of it, can be repaired right in your kitchen. Don't have a kitchen? Find someone who does, and give them this book. Find a community kitchen, or start one.

Early spring, cabbage and arugula go into the raised beds out front.

Honey! Sit down! Have some soup!

Grandmas and Aunties have known this since the dawn of time, but we're gratified to find it's now backed by peer-reviewed studies that point clearly to the connection between eating better and improving mood.[1]

You can, now say the experts, actually lift depression with good food: fruits and vegetables, extra-virgin olive oil, legumes, nuts, wild seafood, whole grains, and *small portions* of grass-fed red meat. Eating this way regulates your inflammatory response, supports the good bacteria in your gut, and makes your brain work better.

Duh! Right?

If you make it yourself from these recipes, you can eat donuts, brownies, mac'n'cheese, and pancakes, along with a bunch of other stuff that would otherwise be totally off limits for a diabetic, a weight watcher, or a heart patient.

You're welcome.

The truth is that everybody would be better off eating this way—not just diabetics and heart patients.

Anybody who wants to feel good, who doesn't want to be diabetic or have a stroke or heart attack or gut problems, needs to eat as if they were a type 2 diabetic and move their buns regularly.

We've all seen the statistics about type 2 diabetes climbing steadily and threatening to consume our already-struggling healthcare system. We know roughly one-third of the population of the U.S. is obese, about a third is diabetic, and about two-thirds are overweight.[2] And in spite of the fact that there's a clear connection between not eating home-cooked food and being overweight or obese, we also know that a fairly low percentage of Americans cook. The bookstores are full of every imaginable kind of cookbook, people collect cookbooks, everybody is bingeing on TV cooking shows, but not that many actually cook their own food.

May we suggest, humbly, that the recipes in this book are going to help keep you and your numbers looking great. Whether you choose the vegetarian or vegan route or include some meat, dairy, and fish in your diet, here's what we're talking about:

- no added sugar
- little or no wheat or gluten or processed grains
- no "bad" fat; limited "good" fat
- only high-quality protein: nuts, seeds, beans, peas, grass-fed meats, wild-caught fish, pasture-raised eggs from extremely happy, well-adjusted chickens
- lots of leafy vegetables
- more vegetables
- did we mention vegetables?
- fruit, mostly fresh, in reasonable amounts: the whole fruit and nothing but the fruit

In other words, *real food, mostly plants*. In his wonderful book, *Food Rules*, Michael Pollan adds "not too much." What you find when you eat this way, though, is that it's hard to eat too much. When you eat real, whole food, your belly gets full. You leave the table feeling like you've had plenty.

Now, I think of my diabetes diagnosis so many years ago as a gift. What I got from it was deep concern and curiosity about what I could do to remain as healthy as possible as long as possible.

Type 2 diabetes, in its early stages, is easy to ignore, easy to live with, and pretty much symptom-free. As a consequence, most folks don't know they have it until they've had it for years, during which time their internal organs have been slowly and subtly deteriorating. By the time they are experiencing symptoms—neuropathy, thirst, frequent urination, fatigue—a lot of damage has been done over a long time.

What happens, too, is that a big part of managing the disease is changing eating habits and exercising: two things most adults—particularly over-weight adults over the age of 50 or so—don't want to do. Folks are okay with having to take a pill or two, or even a shot of insulin, so long as they don't actually have to stop eating the way they like to eat, or get out of their chair and go for a vigorous walk. Particularly when we've worked hard and long, we tend to feel like those biscuits, fried chicken, and Cheerwine are our due—our *birthright*, gosh darn it. We'd much rather watch someone run a marathon on the tube than go out and do a couple of miles ourselves.

Why it's a swell idea to cook and eat this way whether you're diabetic or not.

It's easy.

Yes, you have to chop some stuff and throw some things in a pot or casserole. But it's not complicated or fussy, and requires zero time perfecting knife technique or velvet sauce.

It's not a fad.

There are a few slightly new twists, but for the most part, this has all been around for a long time, and will not be debunked next year when some new study comes out. It's just good, whole food.

It's cheap.

Let's not even count how much you save by not eating out. Let's not even rant about how much really bad fish and chips with horrible, sugary coleslaw can set you back. If you're going to eat out, eat something wonderful in a good place: don't grab crappy food because you can't make something way better. You *can* make something way better, for way less.

It's not wasteful.

The best foods are not wrapped in plastic and cardboard.

You'll be healthier.

When you eat this way, you'll be removing the major causes of inflammation and a number of serious, chronic health problems from your diet. You will actually be nourishing yourself.

Your friends will be impressed.

If the occasion arises for you to feed your pals, they will find out one more thing about you they love. You can cook! They don't need to know how easy it was.

You'll feel better.

When your belly doesn't hurt, isn't bloated, and your energy improves, it's easier to get out for that walk. Then you feel even better. You're more fun when you're not bloated and crabby.

Your food will look and taste better.

Once you get in the habit of eating colorful, fragrant food that delights you, it's hard to go back to beige.

You'll look better.

Way better. Eating this way will improve your skin, your hair, and your shape, without going hungry or depriving yourself.

You'll be happier.

If saving money, saving the planet, improving your social life, feeling better, enjoying your food more, and looking better doesn't make you happy, how about this: peer-reviewed studies now confirm that eating this way actually helps lift depression.[1]

If you're diabetic, or might be, this is for you.

If you haven't been diagnosed yet, chances are one in four that you will by the time you're 65.[3] You know it has to do with your blood glucose being higher than "normal," and you know it means you're not supposed to eat the way you used to. And maybe you're the model patient who tests your blood sugar several times a day, has read those books about the biochemistry of it all, and really understands what's going on in your liver and kidneys. But we're betting NOT. We're betting you kinda know some stuff, and kinda stay on top of your numbers, but mostly DON'T. Which is why we're going to spell things out in a more direct way, skipping all the intracellular activity and all the biochemical theory, and moving right into what you DO about what you have.

It would be amazing if a medical professional could convey much of anything to you within the 15 minutes you're allotted for your appointment. It would be even more amazing if you could retain any of the information you're given during that 15 minutes.[4] Most people don't. Most amazing of all would be if you had the good luck to be seen by a physician who specialized in type 2 diabetes, who had outstanding communication skills, or who believed you would really do what they tell you. Most patients don't.

When you get your diagnosis, you may be referred to a class which involves some PowerPoint presentations about livers and kidneys and islet cells and things. During which, of course, all you can think about is "NO MORE DONUTS?? AAAAAAUGH!" which tends to reduce your receptivity to all the knowledge that instructor worked so hard to get certified to convey to you.

Their challenge (and mine) is trying to help you understand a disease you can neither see nor feel until it has already done damage.

Let's boil it down:
YOUR BODY CAN'T PROCESS OR USE THE
FOOD YOU ARE STUFFING INTO IT, AND AS A
RESULT YOU ARE KILLING YOURSELF, WHICH
WILL ONLY BE OBVIOUS WHEN IT'S TOO
LATE AND YOUR EYES, FINGERS, TOES, AND
KIDNEYS START TO GO.

Did your doctor make that clear? If they really
got through to you, and you truly understand, why is
your blood glucose still sky high and your HgA1c way
over your target? Hmmmm?

We'd like to suggest that instead of thinking
of it as a disease, a bad thing, why not think of it as a
clever genetic adaptation your body benefits from?
Why not see it as just the excuse you need to do all
the things everyone should be doing anyway?

You, my diabetic friend, have a system that
has been adapted to running on very little fuel. Lean
fuel, in fact. You have been equipped to survive on
practically nothing—twigs and leaves. That would be
cool in a post-apocalyptic situation, but of course,
not cool when everyone around you is chomping on
Cinnabons and slugging down Coca-Cola.

You may not be able to reverse damage that's
already done, but you can stop the damage from
increasing. There are plenty of us who have taken
ourselves from consistently high blood glucose
readings and HgA1c results back down into normal,
non-diabetic range without medications.

Here's what the medical experts say.

Here it is, abbreviated, straight from the Mayo Clinic:
*"Healthy lifestyle choices can help prevent type 2
diabetes...even if you have diabetes in your family. If
you've already received a diagnosis of diabetes, you
can use healthy lifestyle choices to help prevent compli-
cations. If you have prediabetes, lifestyle changes can
slow or stop the progression to diabetes."* [5]

And, from the American Diabetes Association:
*"Get more physical activity...Get plenty of fiber...Go for
whole grains...Lose extra weight...Skip fad diets and
just make healthier choices."* [6]

You'll notice there's nothing from the Mayo
Clinic or American Diabetes Association's main
message that says "don't eat sugar" or "lose the
animal fat," or for that matter, exactly how to eat to
lower your blood sugar. So we're gonna fill in some
gaps about avoiding sugar, limiting fats, and making
"healthier choices."

It's pretty clear that the way most folks put on weight is by eating foods specifically designed to make you want more. Processed carbohydrates, plus sugar and salt, are easy and cheap to make, ship, buy, and eat. They also pack more calories with less nutrition than natural, "whole" foods. So whether or not you think those carbohydrate molecules and sugar molecules are dangerous, there's no argument that they are behind weight gain, and weight gain is behind most type 2 diabetes. Lose ten pounds, and you'll see it in your blood glucose numbers immediately. Get your weight down to "normal" range, and your numbers will often, if not always, start to look "normal," too.

Start with brownies, donuts, pancakes, and macaroni and cheese.

There is so much hazy, weasel-wordy information out there about a "healthy lifestyle," even from big medical organizations, that it's really tough to sort your way through. Then there are the folks who want to tell you about what a carbohydrate molecule looks like, or what, exactly, your pancreas does. Everything, in fact, except what you really need to know, which is, WHAT THE HECK CAN I EAT??

More important, **you need to find strategies for not only feeding yourself well, but making it work for your whole family.** It's one thing—a big thing—for you to adopt a sugar-free, whole-food, plant-based way of eating. Getting your exhausted spouse, stuck-in-the-eighties parents, housemates, or eye-rolling kids to go along is another thing altogether. That's why you'll find lots of familiar food—comfort food—in this book. The deal is, if it's donuts or brownies or pancakes or mac'n'cheese, and it looks like donuts or brownies or pancakes or mac'n'cheese, only it tastes better than other pancakes or mac'n'cheese, who cares if it's great, plant-based, healthy, sugar-free food? Don't announce what's in it, or not in it, just *put it out there*. In a perfect world, you'll be able to put a meal on the table that works for everybody, including you.

Blackberries, whipped coconut cream, page 165, and Mimi's Badass Brownies, page 58.

A couple of years ago, watching and listening to physician after physician from all over the world present a mountain of data, I had to rethink what I thought I'd known about diabetes prevention and control. According to every single presenter at the 2019 Plantricians Conference, a gathering in Oakland, California, of more than 1,000 physician experts from all over the world, it wasn't carbs that were the big problem. It's animal fat that is the biggest obstacle preventing your body from metabolizing glucose. That, in addition to the overload of processed carbs from processed food, is why most of us are diabetic. To someone like me who had been religiously avoiding carbs for decades, but helping myself to as much meat and cheese as I wanted, that was not a message I expected or wanted to hear.

On the way back home, head spinning from five days of nonstop PowerPoint presentations, I announced to my husband, as he navigated downtown Oakland and pointed us south, toward home, that I was going vegan. I had decided to run an experiment on myself, completely eliminating meat, fish, and dairy from my diet. There was a thoughtful silence. Then he said, "I'm in."

We were both astonished at how easy it was, and how many side benefits there were. Could I, who never met a pork chop or grilled rib or London broil I didn't like, suddenly and completely give them up? No more creamy blue cheese? No more *any* cheese? In a word, yes. Did I have cravings? Once in a while, for a burger or a hit of whipped cream. But the rewards were almost immediate, and I quickly figured out how to deal with the burger craving with non-meat burgers.

Six months later, I had lost a few pounds and brought my HgA1c down three points, from 7.3 to 7. As she shared the lab results with me, my physician said "that just doesn't happen in people your age." But it did. Not by eating fewer carbs, but by eliminating animal fat completely.

How did it work for my husband? He lost some weight. His stomach flattened. He felt great. His skin looked great. He also started cooking more, because he was intrigued with the idea of making every meal colorful and not boring. Would I call that a success? Would you? Thought so.

If you have any questions about whether or not the "plant-based" idea is solid advice, please check out the "What to Read" section, along with recommendations for "What to Watch" in the back of this book or on LynneBowman.com.

One of the few things we do have good, science-based, peer-reviewed evidence of in the field of nutrition, is that the more plants you eat, the healthier you are. There's lots of science behind recommending that you eat mostly plants—lots of leaves, especially—and if you do eat dairy or meat, make sure it's in limited quantities and of the highest quality. (See "Where to Shop" on page 188.) This is how you'll save the world along with your internal organs: by not eating factory-farmed meat, poultry, and dairy, you're reducing groundwater pollution, reducing the overuse of antibiotics, reducing carbon emissions, reducing plastic use, and greatly improving the lives of pigs, cows, and chickens, as well as your own.

Is "plant-based" another food fad that will be gone in a year or two?

No. You can't really call something that's been working well for people since the dawn of time a fad.

But while we're at it, let's talk about food fads.

In 1967, it was the Metrecal diet, replacing three meals a day with a syrupy, nasty chocolate milky drink, in a can. Fortunes were made as every female in sight who thought she was five pounds overweight went for it. In those days, don't forget, you were fired from your job as a "stewardess" on any airline if, at your weekly weigh-in, you were over your regulation weight. For a woman 5'6" tall, it was 125 pounds. If you look at photos of women on the street in, say, 1962, most were slender by today's standards, and struggling to stay that way.

In 1968, I was way over my head managing the advertising department of Redken Laboratories, then a new, small, innovative hair products company in Van Nuys, California. Determined, at the age of 21 or 22, to stay model-thin, I followed the latest 800-calorie-a-day rage, the name of which I don't remember. What I do remember is going to work on nothing but half a banana and a few ounces of skim milk, and promptly fainting.

My official Redken Laboratories head shot, about 1968.

After that, it was the Stillman Diet: all meat and dairy, virtually no carbs. Did it work? Yes, you lost weight. Was it good for your liver, kidneys, digestive system? Um, no. But in those days, being healthy wasn't a thing. Being beautiful and skinny was a thing. Now that I think about it, it's amazing we survived those crazy diets, along with the other bad decisions we were making. It must have been all that great music and nights at the Palomino Club. I'm remembering Tony Booth, a pal who led the house band there for years, giving me a disapproving once-over one evening, pronouncing me "too skinny. Your legs look like sticks." I was thrilled, of course, to be "too skinny."

By the '70s, though, something had shifted in the food universe. People were reading Adelle Davis, M.F.K. Fisher, and watching Julia Child master the art of French cooking, then buying her books. In 1971, in Berkeley, California, Alice Waters and Paul Aratow opened Chez Panisse, and helped revolutionize the way we see cooking, food, and restaurants. We hipsters were growing up, having families, and beginning to see the supermarket as something our parents' generation loved, but we now knew better. We were planting gardens, taking Lamaze classes, making our own baby food, wearing a lot of calico.

In the '80s, a lot of us moved from flour sack prints to suits with shoulder pads, but the food revolution marched on, now joined with the microcomputer. The '90s brought the Internet: a whole new batch of food fads and a tsunami of nutrition advice, most of it not so great.

Now, here we are, 40 years into all things digital, with the ability to have a car or a meal appear at our door on demand with a few keystrokes, and we're fatter than ever. Enough with the fads.

Top right: Another me, 1974, during a blonde period on staff at an ad agency in Winston-Salem, North Carolina.

Bottom right: Here we were in 1978 in Stanfield, North Carolina.

I know you. If it's not fairly simple, you won't mess with it.

Everything we look at, touch and hear these days is too complicated, and we all have way too much to do. Cooking and eating should not be complicated. The simpler, the better.

Nobody needs 100 recipes. Or 50, for that matter. What you need to know is how to get through today, and maybe this week. Whether you've recently been given some bad news about your blood glucose numbers, or are just trying to eat smarter, what you probably want are a few reliable, go-to ideas for easy things you can keep in the fridge or throw together when you stumble in the door at night, or are trying to get out the door in the morning.

The recipes in this book completely eliminate added sugar and only include wheat in sourdough bread. There are a few, gluten-free processed carbs here and there. There are lots of vegetables, plenty of fiber, and some good protein. There will also be some good, healthy fat in most of these dishes, because you do need some fat. Not much. Some.

Most of us don't like to count carbs or calories or even measure anything. This is a cookbook, after all, so there are measurements, but use them as guides, and don't worry too much if, like me, you're a bit sloppy in the kitchen.

The idea is for you to have fun and not get your panties all in a bunch.

The recipes in this book are mostly three to five ingredients, maybe one or two more. Hardly anything (except the baking) has to be done precisely the way it's written. Most of us love to riff a bit as we go along, and that's as it should be. Have fun. Fail. Try it again. Most of these recipes are also great to cook with kids, or let the kids do on their own.

We'll leave it to other people to go on and on about how your pancreas works, or doesn't. What we hope to do here is help you make some new habits with great-tasting, easy things that are fast and forgiving to make, so you'll actually make them, eat them, and serve them to your grateful friends and family, who will be happy eating what you eat, which will be a good thing for you and your friends and family. Or people you don't even know yet who live around the corner or one floor above you.

This book is meant to encourage you to not just watch but to cook. It's full of old-timey family favorites, plus some that may not be familiar at all to you. Something old and something new. Everything easy. All of it is good food, real food, which is perfectly fine for folks with a number of different health issues. It's all diabetic-friendly, either gluten-free or can be, dairy-free or can be, plant-based, even mostly vegan. And it's all just as healthy for the soil, the air, the planet, as it is for you. Who knew you could save yourself, your family, and the earth with brownies and donuts? *Let's do this.*

This sign, on the wall at the Healthy Habit in Auburn, California, pretty much says it all.

3 WORD DIET

eat · real · food

Here's how.

1. **Sit down when you eat.**

   In a chair, at a table, on a rock, on some grass, on the beach. Not in your car, if you can possibly help it.

2. **Eat leafy things two or three times a day.**

   Don't freak. It's easy, once you know how. Make the pesto on page 105, and put it on nearly anything, or just eat it by the spoonful: it's a concentrated shot of dark greens. You'll find plenty of other ways to eat leaves, raw and cooked, in this book: smoothies, coleslaw, salsa verde, salads, soups.

3. **Replace sugar.**

   If you have to eat something from a package, read the ingredients part of the nutrition label. Aloud, if you can. Is there any form of sugar in the ingredients? Don't eat or drink it. Find the healthy, good-tasting sweeteners that work for you (page40) and use them.

4. **Eat veggies at every meal.**

   Like eating leaves, this is a habit that will, literally, save your life. *Half of every meal should be veggies.* Every time you sit down (#1, above) to eat, make sure your plate passes the test. No? See #2.

5. **Always carry emergency food.**

   It's so easy to have a small bag of nuts or some fruit with you, and it will keep you out of trouble.

6. **Eat before you meet.**

   Whether it's a staff meeting, a kindergarten potluck, or a black-tie deal, don't go on an empty stomach. Bad decisions are born of hunger. Dig into your stash of emergency food before you get there, and you'll be able to pass up those weenies-in-a-blanket without a thought.

7. Stick with basic black.

No sugar, no milk, no cream, no latte, no frappahootie anything. I took a class with my buddy Lisa once about how to start a cafe, and the very first thing the instructor said was, "You have to understand that you won't be in the coffee business, you'll be in the milk and sugar business." Peet's, Starbucks, and the rest are selling milk and sugar. When you go in, and of course you will go in, know that you don't want that milk and sugar. You want good, black coffee or tea. If you still really, really want that creamy, sweet taste, use non-dairy milk (oat, soy, coconut, etc.) and non-sugar sweetener. Buy your favorite sweetener (page 40) in packets, and always have them with you. In case you were wondering, Lisa and I lost interest in starting a cafe when we found out how much work it is. Fortunately, some other pals opened up Downtown Local, the most brilliant little cafe ever, in Pescadero, so we were off the hook.

8. Eat your fruit whole.

(Except a splash of 100% cranberry; see page 39) You already know this if you've ever been on any kind of diet. A glass of orange juice is the equivalent of eating a bunch of oranges, but without the fiber. A whole orange is a great idea; a glass of juice is not.

Miss H, here about nine years old, shows us how.

9. **Eat early.**

   Try to be completely done eating by 5 p.m. or earlier. *Whaaaaat?* I can hear you screaming all the way out here in the redwoods. You need to at least try, for two extremely important reasons. First, you'll sleep better (See #10). Second, your digestive system, which is most active mid-day, will be allowed to do its job, so you will be getting more energy from the food you eat and less stored fat. There is a long explanation for why this is so, but I don't have time here, and neither do you.

10. **Sleep.**

    Doesn't do you any good to eat beautifully if you're going to stay up half the night working, fretting, binge watching, or texting. Go to bed and sleep at least seven hours, eight hours would be better, and more is fine. For your blood glucose, skin, relationships, mood, healing, everything, you have to sleep. *Your body can only heal and cleanse itself while you sleep.* Put yourself to sleep reading or listening to *Why We Sleep*, by Mathew Walker, PhD. Check out the Pro Sleeping Tips on page 192. If you've done some exercise during the day, something like 30-45 minutes of walking, dancing, yoga, pilates, cycling, whatever, you're two-thirds of the way to blissful sleep. The other third is making sure you eat for better sleep.

11. **Read. The. Label. Always.** If it even has a label, it's suspect.

12. **Go ahead and cheat. A little.**

    Would a few drops of real maple syrup on your pumpkin pancakes be the end of the world? Absolutely not. In fact, the hope is that by staying with these guidelines pretty faithfully, when you do break them, it will be lovely.

Sleeping quarters at Old Dog Farm.

At left, dear reader, is the actual kitchen table that is the nerve center of Old Dog Farm. I spend a huge amount of my time on that couch at the foot of the stairs, eating, thinking, reading, and yakking. The table and six matching chairs, now in another room, were purchased for $49 (plus sales tax) at Habitat Restore, a thrift store run by Habitat for Humanity. The couch under all those pillows was $250 (plus tax) at a local consignment store: it's bombproof and wipe-offable. The pillows in washable zip-off covers were mostly from T.J.Maxx, $15-$20 a piece. The mercury lamps? I went crazy over them in a friend's house, so she unplugged them and gave me the pair. The chandelier? Gift from a guy whose wife hated it. (Go figure!) The gray turtleback chair was rescued from an elderly family member and recovered with indoor-outdoor fabric. The white tablecloth is made out of old Clorox bottles, so you can't stain it and don't need to iron it. When we sit around the table—friends, kids, committee members, family, or folks I just met—I hope they feel they can laugh too loud or spill their juice or wine and it's perfectly fine. I hope they also understand at some level that it's a holy place, crumbs, stains, and all.

You need a table. Small is fine. It will help you be more selective about your guests.

This little table, from an unfinished furniture store, marked down (always!), was painted with sample pots left over from choosing various wall colors. It can seat four or five in a pinch, and has been the scene for lots of good meals, chess games, and the radio shows buddy Catherine and I record for KPDO, our local Pescadero radio station.

We've come now to a place where many homes don't even have a kitchen table, or a dining room table, or any table at all where a small group can sit and eat. And while I revere it as a custom and a tradition and a lovely thing to do, I'm going to admit to you right here and now that it takes some effort to put a real meal on the table, even a humble one. It takes planning, time, and work. Not that it's punishment, but we just haven't left time in our days and nights to do it anymore. If you're commuting to work, have a kid or two and an extra-curricular activity or two...how many hours is that every week, just in the car? No wonder folks opt to just drive through and fuel up at some awful pre-fab grab-it place. To do otherwise has become something against the grain.

May I submit to you, dear pals, that we should hang on to our tables and all that goes with them. Your table is where your kids learn everything worth knowing, from you. It's where you feed one another emotionally as well as culturally. It's where you demonstrate respect to your kids, along with sharing and listening and gratitude and so many other things.

Plus, being around the table with people you love is more fun than anything. It's the best. Not true for you? Maybe it's time for some new people.

In just this past year, so many meal delivery options are now springing up to bring good quality prepared, or partially prepared, food to your door that you do have possibilities to eat well at home that didn't exist not too long ago. When you do order in, if you can, don't forget to make the table a welcoming and beautiful place to eat.

Make room in your kitchen for real food.
Get rid of all the crap.

I know there are experts who would disagree and tell you to take "baby steps." If that's more your style, great. But it's not mine.

Having crammed cupboards or a stuffed refrigerator doesn't help you put good food on the table. Just like having too many clothes stuffed in your closet, an overstuffed fridge gets in your way.

Does that food contain bleached white flour in any form? Ditch it. Sugar? Just no. Ingredients you can't pronounce or don't recognize? Out. Anything on the label that says "healthy" or "natural" or "wholesome"? Bye-bye. Anything in the fridge that's been opened more than a week or two? Gone. Anything in the pantry you bought more than a year or so ago? Gone.

Let's talk about those "nutrition facts" on labels.
The truth, according to T. Colin Campbell and others, is that reducing foods to their chemical pieces and parts is very dicey business.[7] Two different carrots, for one simple example, depending on where they're grown, how they're grown, how and when they're harvested and processed, will have two very different sets of nutritional "facts." These values can vary not just slightly but by as much as eight or ten times. Coming up with a precise measurement of any particular nutritional component for any food is a guess. An educated guess, but still a guess. In other words, those "nutrition facts" aren't dead-on about nutrition, and they're not necessarily facts.

How those components react in your particular body is another variable that can't be accounted for in numbers on a nutritional label. **They're included in this book for you to have, when and if those numbers matter to you.** It is interesting to see, if you want to compare, just how much more fiber or protein or whatever some of these recipes have compared to more conventional recipes. Our friends who need to keep close tabs on potassium or sodium, per doctors' orders, will have those values, as closely as we can calculate them, on each recipe. You pals of the keto or paleo persuasion will also have your protein and carb numbers. The rest of us can pretty much forget all the counting, so long as what we're putting in our bodies is good stuff.

How to read a nutrition label.

First, of course, get a good grip on how big a chunk they're talking about. What exactly is that serving size? And who, exactly, eats only a tablespoon of anything?

Calories: Yes, the total you consume in a normal day has consequences. But even more important is how much actual nutrition is in those calories.

Saturated fat: A thing you don't really want. If most of the fat is saturated, move on.

Cholesterol: What is a safe and healthy "%DV" (daily value)? Nobody knows for sure. So 0% is good. If you're not eating meat or dairy, you're not eating cholesterol.

Sodium: Watch it, if your doc says so.

Total Carbs: If you're diabetic, dietitians usually prescribe 30-45 carbs max per meal. Less is good.

Added Sugars: This should be 0. If there are added sugars, put the package down.

Protein: What's desirable here depends on who you talk to. It's most often calculated on body weight and activity level, so 45-55 grams a day minimum for average-size sedentary women on the lower end, and men on the higher end.

Vitamins and Minerals: This is important if you are on certain prescribed medications, or dialysis, for example, which requires that you keep potassium at a certain level.

Ingredients: This is the important bit. What, exactly, is in this food? If the list is longer than six to eight ingredients, read it carefully. It is supposed to be in order of the most prevalent ingredient, first, to the least, last. If it's hard to spell, pronounce, or understand, it's likely not something great for you.

Aging apple trees, like this one at Old Dog Farm, produce fruit with a nutritional profile that will vary a lot from the apples you see in grocery stores.

Nutrition Facts

3 servings per container
Serving size — 1/3 container (100g) (makes about 1 cup)

	Per serving	%DV*		%DV*
Calories	290		88	
Total Fat	9g	12%	27g	35%
Sat. fat	3.5g	18%	11g	55%
Trans Fat	0g		0g	
Cholest.	0mg	0%	0mg	0%
Sodium	580mg	25%	1750mg	76%
Total Carb.	49g	18%	146g	53%
Fiber	2g	7%	6g	21%
Total Sugars	1g		2g	
Incl. Added Sugars	0g	0%	1g	2%
Protein	4g		12g	
Vitamin D	0mcg	0%	0mcg	0%
Calcium	185mg	15%	555mg	45%
Iron	1mg	6%	3mg	15%
Potassium	90mg	2%	271mg	6%

*The % Daily Value (DV) tells you how much a nutrient in a serving of food contributes to a daily diet. 2,000 calories a day is used for general nutrition advice.

INGREDIENTS: BROWN RICE PASTA (BROWN RICE, RICE BRAN, WATER), FILTERED WATER, TAPIOCA STARCH, EXPELLER PRESSED: CANOLA AND/OR SAFFLOWER OIL, COCONUT OIL, SALT, PEA PROTEIN, VEGAN NATURAL FLAVORS, TRICALCIUM PHOSPHATE, CANE SUGAR, LACTIC ACID (VEGAN), XANTHAN GUM, YEAST EXTRACT, TITANIUM DIOXIDE COLOR (NATURALLY OCCURING MINERAL), ANNATTO COLOR, ONION.

NUTRITION FACTS

6 servings per container
Serving size — 2oz. (57g)

Amount per serving		% Daily Value*
Calories	210	
Total Fat 2g		3%
Saturated Fat 0g		0%
Trans Fat 0g		
Cholesterol 0mg		0%
Sodium 0mg		0%
Total Carbohydrate 44g		16%
Dietary Fiber 2g		7%
Total Sugars 0g		
Includes 0g Added Sugars		0%
Protein 5g		
Vitamin D 0mcg		0%
Calcium 10mg		0%
Iron .7mg		4%
Potassium 160mg		4%

The % Daily Value (DV) tells you how much a nutrient in a serving of food contributes to a daily diet. 2,000 calories a day is used for general nutrition advice.

INGREDIENTS:
Organic Brown Rice Flour, Water.

Does it say sugar in any way?

PUT THAT PACKAGE DOWN AND MOVE ON.

Here, to refresh your memory, are just some of the ways they say "sugar" when they don't want you to know just how much of it is in that food: Dextrose. Fructose. Galactose. Glucose. Lactose. Maltose. Sucrose. Agave nectar. Barley malt syrup. Beet sugar. Brown rice syrup. Brown sugar. Cane crystals (or cane juice crystals). Cane sugar. Coconut sugar or coconut palm sugar. Barley malt. Blackstrap molasses. Brown rice syrup. Buttered sugar/buttercream. Caramel. Carob syrup. Corn syrup. Evaporated cane juice. Fruit juice. Fruit juice concentrate. Golden syrup. High-fructose corn syrup. Honey. Invert sugar. Malt syrup. Maple syrup.

It's all sugar. And sugar is not your friend.

You'll need a stove.

It doesn't have to be huge or crazy expensive. It just needs to work. And what about that stunning-but-sensible backsplash? Thank you for noticing. A tin piece from the exterior of an old building that was demolished in Chicago, purchased at the San Francisco Garden Show many years ago. Yes, tested it for lead in the paint, and we're good. If you're going to spend some time here, at your range top, with your snoot in a pot, make it as wonderful as you can.

Make friends with a microwave.

No, it won't fry your brain, regardless what your pal—the one who always has an electronic device held close to her ear—says.[8] You can be forgiven for being skeptical, but I'm a microwave fan. Not for cooking, exactly, but for heating and reheating. Melting. Defrosting. I like a microwave with as few controls as possible, along the lines of "on" and "off" and "1 minute." Then you just keep punching the 1-minute button until it's about as many minutes as you want.

So, when you see an instruction to "nuke" something, that's what we're talking about. Why do we call it "nuking"? I'm not sure how that got started, but it's probably some hideous political thing. When you find out, let me know, and it will go in the next book.

Salt is beautiful.

It comes in different flavors, great colors, even black, and it's sparkly. Why hide it? Put it out where you can play with it. You need a little wooden spoon to serve the salt with, because it will corrode a metal spoon. Found that out the hard way. And, like salsa verde, salt makes most everything better, so sprinkle some on. If you're not eating processed food that's full of salt—fast food, packaged food, crappy food from the end aisles at Safeway—you don't need to worry about adding a few grains to the food you're making.

If you have high blood pressure, ignore this "salt is beautiful" pitch, please, and do what your doc tells you to do, which is probably "no salt."

If you're going to use salt, make it good. Next time you have ten minutes (we can dream!) just look at all those little jewels on the shelf at Williams Sonoma or some other gourmet kitchen store. Treat yourself to at least one.

Salts you throw in the pot, while you're cooking: unflavored white salts, kosher flake salt.

Salts you sprinkle on your food, after it's cooked, and show off on your table: flavored, colorful salts—truffle, smoky, pink Himalayan.

Oils. Also beautiful. In moderation.

There's a lot of discussion these days about which oils are better for what. Unless you really want to nerd out about it, it boils down to keeping coconut oil on hand for baking and cooking, and good olive oil (fresh, "virgin" olive oil) for salads, pastas, and a few other things.

If you're eating nut butters, nuts, avocados, and seeds, you're getting lots of good vegetable fats. Fish like anchovies and salmon have beneficial oily fats in them. It's animal fat from meat, poultry, and dairy products that are the problem, largely because of the way those animals are fed and medicated.

Why you might want to ditch dairy completely.

There's a simple way to find out if it's worth it for you. You can see logically that milk and cheese and sour cream and scrambled eggs with cheddar are high in saturated, "bad" fat, and high in calories. You may also understand that those factory-farmed dairy items also come with additional toxins you should be concerned about. But the best way to answer the question for yourself (after you've done some reading from page 198) as to whether or not it's worth giving up your favorite gooey cheesy delights is to do it. Try it, for a week, or a month. Are your guts happier? Coughing and runny nose stopped? Acid reflux improved? Did you drop some weight? How does your skin look? Okay, then. Now you know. If only you could see how happy your liver is!

"Meatless meats" and non-dairy butters can help.

A lot of us who make the transition away from meat and dairy use the new meatless meat-like products to get us through: Impossible Burger, Beyond Burger, and the like. After you've tried a few, you may find one or two you like, as part of a burger with everything, or in a pasta dish, where the sauce or fixings are the focus. Throw some of your homemade pesto (page 105) on frozen "meatless meatballs" you've heated up, and you've got a good meal, over pasta, or on their own.

What happens to many of us on the path to fabulousness is that you really do, incredibly, lose your taste for fatty meats and dairy. As you replace brown and beige foods with colorful plant foods and more variety in seasoning, meat and dairy become less appealing. Your taste changes.

There are now vegan butters on the market that you could not identify in a blind test as "fake." They taste fresher, in fact, than packaged "real" butter. Read the labels, and be sure you're happy with the ingredients as well as the taste.

CRANBERRY SPARKLER

Have a drink. Our house specialty: Cranberry Sparkler
While all your less-evolved, less-conscious pals are swilling overpriced, inferior house wines and pretentious cocktails, you'll be drinking and serving this. To everybody. Kids, too. It's pink, it's bubbly: what's not to like?

We've put this recipe up front, in the hope you'll make it for yourself, sit down, and have it in hand as you read the rest of this book, planning your kitchen (and health) triumphs.

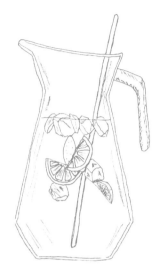

ingredients

100% cranberry juice
(read the label: no sugar!)
—a splash

Fresh lemon and/or lime
juice—half a lemon per glass,
or more

Sparkling mineral water, to
fill the glass or pitcher

Lemon and/or lime slices in it
to make it pretty

If you like it sweeter, add a
pinch or two of your favorite
sweetener (page 40).

Get real with "fake" sugars.

Not sure about kicking sugar completely? Read up from references on page 198, and watch a documentary or two on the subject. It may be the most important thing you do for your health. If you're diabetic or overweight, finding a way to eat sweets that you love that aren't made of sugar is going to go a long way toward meeting your health goals. Think desserts can't possibly be as good without "real" cane sugar? This book is dedicated to persuading you otherwise. You may be surprised at how much better the sugar replacements are now than they were a few years back. Once you start using them, you may realize that it's cane sugar that leaves an aftertaste, makes you thirsty, and isn't what you really want. It isn't what anybody who wants to be healthy really wants.

Since taste buds and noses (largely responsible for how you taste things) are different, here are a few you'll want to try, if you haven't already.

Monk Fruit

A small melon found in the tropical and subtropical regions of South East Asia, monk fruit is said to support the immune system, digestive tract, glands, and respiratory system. Most of the recipes in this book that require sweetener were created or tested with monk fruit sweetener. It's slightly sweeter than sugar, adds virtually no calories or carbs, doesn't leave an aftertaste, and works just like sugar in recipes. It's an all-natural, calorie-free sweetener with zero glycemic index. What's not to like? It comes in powdered, granulated, and "golden" styles, to mimic powdered, granulated, and brown sugars, and is used in about the same measurements as sugar. If you're going for zero carbs, read the label: monk fruit sweeteners are sometimes mixed with erythritol, which has 4 grams of carbs per teaspoon.

Chicory Root (inulin)

My personal favorite, although not always easy to find. Chicory is an herb that grows wild throughout Europe, the United States, and Australia but is also cultivated for culinary use. You may know it as a coffee-like drink popular in New Orleans, but its root is made up of 40 percent inulin, a carbohydrate fiber found naturally in bananas, onions, and wheat, which has made it a favorite for food manufacturers to bulk up the fiber in packaged foods. The inulin in chicory root fiber is also a prebiotic, or a fiber that feeds and promotes the growth of healthy probiotic bacteria in our guts. Foods with natural prebiotics like inulin promote good gut health, and some studies suggest prebiotic additives like inulin from chicory root fiber may improve digestion. You can buy inulin as a sweetener in different forms: my favorite is sold in some health food stores and online as Just Like Sugar, in baking, tabletop and brown sugar varieties. No calories, and only mild, if any, gastric side effects, even in generous amounts.

Fig. 2.—Chicory roots and leaves; *a*, Schlesische variety, root with leaves; *b*, Brunswick and Magdeburg varieties, root. (Both one-sixth natural size.)

Erythritol

A sugar alcohol found in certain fruits, the powdered erythritol you'll find online or in health food stores will most likely contain only about 0.24 calories per gram, or something like 6% of the calories in an equal amount of sugar, with 70% of the sweetness. Erythritol has 4 grams of carbs per teaspoon, but doesn't spike blood sugar or insulin levels and has no effect on blood lipids like cholesterol or triglycerides. It's absorbed into the body from the intestine but eventually excreted from the kidneys unchanged. Although it's considered very safe, as with other sugar alcohols, it can cause digestive issues if you consume too much at a time. Erythritol tastes very much like sugar, although it can have a mild aftertaste. Although erythritol doesn't seem to have any health benefits, it doesn't appear to be harmful in any way and is better tolerated than most other sugar alcohols.

"Swerve" is a brand name sweetener made primarily from erythritol, and is a zero-calorie, non-glycemic product that has no effect on blood glucose or insulin levels. Unlike stevia, it has no bitter aftertaste for most people and measures, browns and caramelizes just like sugar.

Stevia

A natural, zero-calorie sweetener extracted from the leaves of a plant called Stevia rebaudiana, grown for sweetness and medicinal purposes for centuries in South America. It's hundreds of times sweeter than sugar, and has virtually no calories. Some studies suggest stevia can lower high blood pressure in people with hypertension and lower blood sugar levels in people with diabetes. However, not everyone likes the taste of stevia. The flavor depends on the brand, so you may need to experiment to find one you like.

Xylitol

Xylitol is a sugar alcohol with a sweetness similar to sugar, but only 2.4 calories per gram, or about two-thirds of the caloric value of sugar. Xylitol appears to have some benefits for dental health, reducing the risk of cavities and dental decay. Xylitol doesn't raise blood sugar or insulin levels, but, as with other sugar alcohols, it can cause digestive side effects at high doses. **It's also highly toxic to dogs.**

Maltitol

Another sugar alcohol sweetener with similar qualities, used in one of my favorite chocolate products: Trader Joe's "Simply Lite Sugar-Free Chocolate Bars." Tastes great, but three squares is about all you should have at once, or you're likely to experience some gastrointestinal side effects. Used in the frosting for Anytime Brownies or Pumpkin Donuts, however, you'll be getting way less than that on a brownie or two or a donut.

Yacon Syrup

Harvested from the yacon plant, which grows natively in the Andes in South America, this sweetener has recently become popular as a weight loss supplement. It's very high in fructooligosaccharides, which function as soluble fibers that feed the good bacteria in the intestine. Because yacon syrup contains so much soluble fiber, it can help relieve constipation. But, like many of these sweeteners, eating too much at a time can cause digestive problems.

What about coconut sugar, molasses, honey, and maple syrup?

These aren't much different from cane sugar as far as their effect on your blood sugar and calorie count are concerned. They may contain slightly smaller amounts of fructose and some tiny amount of nutrients, but your liver and kidneys really won't be able to tell the difference.

Do not feed me Xylitol

Opposite page: The cooking end of the kitchen at Old Dog Farm. The island had been my father-in-law's desk for 30 years. After that, it served in the garage as a workbench for him, then for my husband. Now, with a stainless steel top, new finish, and thoughtful additions by my pal Cotton, page 117, it's enjoying a glamorous new life at the center of things.

Equip yourself.

It doesn't take a whole lot, but there are certain things you need to have handy to make this all work. Whether you're in that place where you're throwing everything into the street except what truly matters, or moving into your very own space for the first time, here's what you need. Plus, of course—*attitude*— a cook's best tool.

A garden pot or two on your porch or balcony or kitchen window shelf. Grow chives, parsley, basil, nasturtiums, calendulas, wheatgrass—lots of good stuff to throw in a salad or decorate a plate with. Make friends with somebody at your local nursery, and they'll fix you right up and tell you how not to kill your gorgeous, nutritious new babies.

Baking pans in fun shapes. Everything tastes better when it's a cool shape, like a butterfly or a flower. Bundt pans, miniature loaf pans, all good.

Big skillet with a lid. It's hard to beat black cast iron for the skillet, and a glass lid makes it just about perfect for everything. Cast iron is cheap, looks great in the most amazing modern kitchen or out on a cattle drive, and will never wear out. All you need to remember is no soap, ever. Just wash with very hot water and scrub it clean. Small price to pay for a pan you can cook anything in.

If you're someone who has a problem with iron, as in the doctor has said you shouldn't take in too much, get something like Le Creuset (or Staub), which has a coating baked over the iron.

Big soup jar. After you finish this book, you will almost certainly be making a bunch of Genius Soup every week, and you will need something to keep it in: a big glass jar that holds a half a gallon or more with a tight-fitting lid.

Blender. There are pretty good ones out there for the price of a couple of drinks. You only need three speeds and "pulse," but if you want the blend-o-rama one that has the huge glass bowl and 37 speeds, get it. It needs to smush things up, not leak, and look cool on the counter if that's where it's gonna live. There are also single-serving, adorable teeny blenders that let you just put a lid on what you've blended and run to the car with it.

Bowl. Most of us have too many, but if you want to keep it simple, just be sure you have one HUGE bowl. There's no such thing as too big. If you're doing salad or pasta you need to toss it, and you can't do that in an undersized bowl.

Butler's friend. Cheap, small, easy wine bottle opener.

Can opener. One of those cool ones that will pick up the lid for you. Not electric.

Chain mail. Best way to clean your cast iron. It's a metal scrubber in the form of a piece of chain mail, just as if you'd cut it off a knight's sleeve.

Citrus reamer. You'll notice the recipes in this book involve putting lemon, lime, and orange juice in almost everything, so you're going to need a way to squeeze that juice out. If you don't have a squeezie thing you love, get yourself a reamer. They look and feel so cool, and nobody but you will know what it is. Feels great in your hand. Gives you total mastery over that piece of fruit. Wielded aggressively, it will help you put the juice of half a lemon right where it needs to be.

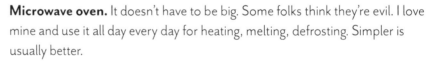

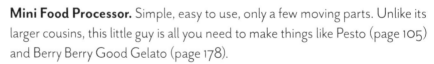

Colander. Something attractive if possible, or at least something with great character. In addition to draining your just-washed produce and pasta, you can just plunk it on the table with pretty fruits or vegetables in it.

Donut baking pan. Doesn't have to be the priciest one, and two are a good idea. Donut recipes start on page 62.

Glass jars with lids. This is how you save all your food, to freeze or refrigerate or put on the shelf. You'll need a variety of sizes, from 4 ounces up to a quart.

Knives. If you only get a couple of things on this list, go for a good knife or two. Small paring knives 4 or 5" long, a serrated bread knife, and a big chopping knife could be enough. Don't put them in the dishwasher and keep them sharp. If you're going to eat well, you're going to have to chop some fruits and vegetables, and if you're going to chop some things, you need a good knife or two.

Measuring spoons. These were a gift from my daughter, Kelly, and I hang them out where I can see them all the time. Your tools can be a pleasure to look at, and to hold.

Microwave oven. It doesn't have to be big. Some folks think they're evil. I love mine and use it all day every day for heating, melting, defrosting. Simpler is usually better.

Mini Food Processor. Simple, easy to use, only a few moving parts. Unlike its larger cousins, this little guy is all you need to make things like Pesto (page 105) and Berry Berry Good Gelato (page 178).

Pyrex (or other heat-proof) glass measuring cups: 8-cup, 4-cup, and 1-cup, with pouring spouts.

Pasta or stockpot. BIG is good; something you can get a gallon or more of soup in.

Potato masher. Great for mashing guacamole and all kinds of things that need to be squished and mashed.

Salad spinner. If you're reading this book, chances are your future includes a lot of salad, and it needs to be dry before you dress it.

Saucepan with a lid that fits well. Fairly heavy, good quality, medium-sized, if you only want to deal with one.

Sheet pan with edges. Fairly heavy, good quality, medium-sized sheet pan with sides is perfect for World's Greatest Granola (page 86).

Soup pot. Any heavy pot with a tight-fitting lid will do, so long as it's big enough for a batch of soup or beans. A big batch. At least a gallon, preferably two gallons.

Spatula. A metal one for your big skillet with a lid, and a plastic one if you're using a nonstick pan.

Spoons. Wooden, slotted, big, maybe a ladle.

Timer. I like a manual timer, in this case, an adorable chicken. In one quick motion, you twist it to where you want it and you're good. No need to clean and dry your fingers so you can use a digital machine.

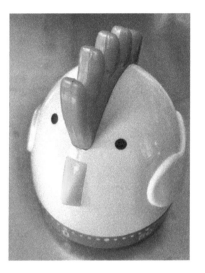

Wooden clothespins. If there ever was a handier thing, we don't know what it is. Clip a book open. Clip a package closed. Clip gloves together. Clip a bunch of little things together. Heck, you can even clip something up to dry.

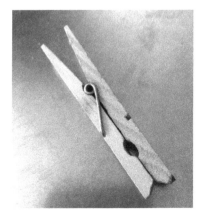

Plan your food day.

Okay, you're all set, right? You've stocked your pantry, got your equipment sorted out. You're ready to dive into these recipes. Awrighty then. Let's talk about what your food day looks like.

Eat the fresh stuff first. Make it a habit to scan for the fresh things that need to be eaten up in the next day or two, then figure out how to get them into your belly.

Do you have to eat breakfast? No. But it's another habit you might want to cultivate, for a couple of reasons. First, because, hey, you can eat brownies for breakfast. Or donuts. Or any of the other good things in this book, so long as you're making them yourself, and know what's in them.

Second, there is some science behind the calories you eat early in the day not counting as much as the calories you eat later in the day. So, eat! Just make sure it's good food, and include vegetables. Smoothies are ideal, especially if they're at least half veggies. Oatmeal is excellent, so long as it's plain old oatmeal, no sugar, with fruit. Make it with soy milk for more protein.

For lunch, every day: A salad with lots of green and as many other colors as possible. Make sure the dressing is something you've made, or are carrying with you, if you're eating out. Or eat that great soup you've made from these recipes, with some fruit or fresh veggies on the side. Every day? Yes. Or salad. No sandwich? Not unless you made it at home with truly good bread.

Dinner: *At least half your plate should be vegetables.* Beans! Lentils! A casserole, salad, or any of the main or side dishes in this book. Or, always, soup. In the mood for a burger? Okay, but make it meatless, smother it with condiments —dill pickle, lettuce, arugula, tomatoes, onions, avocado, Vegenaise—with a side of slaw. Want to really treat yourself or a pal or two for dinner? Simple Salmon, on a bed of Creamy Cauliflower with something green on the side. Or Cowgirl Caviar, made ahead. Beyond fabulous.

To Pam. moved 1971. Fall to Winter Fruit

Stock up.

Stay the heck out of the grocery store completely, if you can. Go once a week or order from a delivery service and don't go at all, unless it's to your local farmer's market. Your life will improve. You'll save money. You won't buy those magazines at the checkout counter. You won't run into people you feel obligated to talk to even though you're late and tired and hungry. Keep yourself stocked up with these indispensables and you'll never be without something swell to eat.

You'll be going to your local farmer's market or produce stand to pick up fresh berries or apricots, fresh greens, and so on. What's listed here are the things you should always keep on hand that won't go bad any time soon.

Almond butter. Creamy or chunky, with or without salt. You can grind it yourself at your local health food store, or buy it from Trader Joe's or Costco, but it doesn't have a super long shelf life, so get it somewhere that has high stock turnover. People who are allergic to all other nuts, by the way, can sometimes eat almonds without a reaction.

Artichoke hearts. In water or oil, glass jars or cans. You're gonna plunk them into pasta, salad, all kinds of things.

Artsy cold-pressed olive oil. Artsy is not the brand, mind you, it's the attitude. Olive oils are just like wine in that they are best when made by people who are proud to put their name on the bottle. They can be as different from one another as wines are, and some are so good that they are all you need, all by themselves, to dress a salad or pasta. Unlike wine, olive oil doesn't improve with age. It needs to be on the fresh side.

Your local farmer's market is a good place to do some tasting, and you might even get to meet the folks growing the olives and squishing them into oil. If it is a fresh, locally cold-pressed olive oil, in addition to being delicious, enjoy the smell, the color, and the way it makes your skin glow. No, it's not cheap, but a little money spent on great olive oil is money very well spent. Anyway, you'll be using it sparingly, in small amounts.

Be sure to store it either in the fridge or some other cool spot, away from your stove or heater. Real food, unlike packaged food full of preservatives, will deteriorate if you don't store it tightly sealed away from light and heat sources.

Baking soda and baking powder. In little cans that seal, not boxes.

Beans. A can or two of black beans, cannellini beans, cut green beans, and some dried lentils, at least. Watch the sodium or stick to dried.

Canned crushed pineapple. We've always got at least one or two cans, just in case we need to make an emergency of-course-I-would-never-forget-your-birth-day cake (page 160).

Canned (or boxed) pumpkin and butternut squash. For donuts, pancakes, and so many other fabulous things: you always want to have some when you need it.

Capers. What ARE these little dudes, anyway? They are, since you ask, the unripened flower buds of *Capparis spinosa* or *Capparis inermis* plants, prickly perennials native to the Mediterranean and some parts of Asia. They are sold by size: the smaller the caper, the more delicate in texture and flavor it is. The smallest ones are usually labeled "non-pareil." They pack a whole lot of fabulous into their tiny little round selves, and they look swell, too.

Cashew butter. Milder flavor than almond butter, used interchangeably with almond butter, and also good as a cheese replacement in some recipes.

Cocoa powder. Make sure there's nothing in it but ground cocoa. "Dutch processed cocoa" is slightly more alkaline and darker in color. The two types can be used interchangeably in these recipes unless you're a complete cocoa nerd.

Coconut oil. Some taste more coconutty than others. Great for greasing baking dishes, frying, and washing your makeup off. Be careful you don't put a bunch down the drain, though, or it will clog your pipes, because it solidifies at room temperature.

Cutting boards. We don't love plastic anything, but a plastic cutting board that can go into the dishwasher is a necessary thing. Plus, of course, a wood cutting board or two that you'll clean with salt. If you eat meat, you need a separate cutting board for meat only. I use Epicurean, which is NOT PLASTIC and can handle dishwasher, 350° heat, and also work as a trivet or pizza board.

Egg replacer. Bob's Red Mill is good, and there are others, usually made from flax seed or arrowroot.

Glucomannan. A soluble, bulk-forming powder from konjac root, which works great as a thickener.

Gluten-free, whole grain pancake mix. Bob's Red Mill is a great brand; there are lots of others.

Lemon pepper. It's been around since the '60s for a reason. Works great on just about everything. Trader Joe's offers a nice grinder version, so it comes out with a lot of fragrance in visible chunks.

Nuts. Raw and/or roasted, salted or not: walnuts, almonds, pistachios, cashews, etc. Nuts have a short shelf life, so refrigerate or freeze them.

Nutritional yeast. Sounds yucky, tastes great. This is deactivated yeast sold as yellow flakes, granules or powder, with a cheesy taste that makes it a great substitute for salty cheeses. It's a good source of B-complex vitamins and has trace amounts of several other vitamins and minerals. Sprinkle it liberally wherever you might use parmesan, guilt-free.

Pasta. Brown rice macaroni, fettuccine noodles, and spaghetti. There are all kinds of interesting new pastas coming out: quinoa, flax—experiment! Taste! I like the way brown rice pasta behaves and tastes.

Pesto. You can buy pretty good pesto in jars to pull out in an emergency. Some are fresh, in the deli case; some are on the condiment shelves and don't need refrigeration. Make some yourself with the recipe on page 105, and freeze it.

Stick freshly cut herbs and edible flowers in a small pot—a creamer works great—of water on the counter, and they'll keep longer and look great. Plus, if it's out there in front of you, you'll remember to use it, which is a great idea.

Parsley is packed with vitamins A and C, along with a long list of other vitamins and minerals, and it adds color, fragrance, and flavor to soups, salads, pasta, and so on. Chop it at the last minute and throw it on.

Produce that keeps well. Jicama, kale, sweet potatoes, celery, lemons, limes, red and yellow peppers, onions, garlic, carrots, parsnips, apples, oranges.

Psyllium. It's just bean husks, and a great way to add fiber to your diet. No flavor, no calories, just a little texture you can hide in nut butter, salad, smoothies, whatever. You can also use it to thicken sauces or cooked fruit without adding calories.

Pumpkin pie spice. Stock up during the holidays, when it's everywhere, so you always have some for pumpkin pancakes or pumpkin donuts.

Salsa verde. A few jars of good green salsa in your larder and you're prepared for all kinds of things. Two tablespoons of it is 10 calories, if that matters, but the point is, it's all vegetables—mostly tomatillos—plus a bit of salt. There's practically nothing this stuff can't do. Eggs, fish, dips, pasta, soup. Go ahead and bloop it on, generously. It makes everything better.

Smoky salt. If salt doesn't agree with you or you're having blood pressure issues, you'll want to skip this paragraph. If you do like salt, get good salt that adds more than just sodium to whatever you're preparing. A good smoky-flavored salt is terrific, for example, on a salad made with tomatoes and lettuce, because you get the fragrance and taste of bacon—subtle, but definitely there—without the bacon. Now, when you go to buy this stuff online or at your local gourmet or organic food store, we don't want you dropping into a dead faint when you see the price. (How much?? For SALT??) Just think of it as an investment in your health and social currency. GREAT GIFT: a big box of Kosher flake salt for cooking.

Spices. *Pumpkin pie spice, always.* Plus cinnamon, nutmeg, curry, pepper, oregano, turmeric, paprika, herbs de Provence, tarragon, at least.

Sugar-free chocolate. Trader Joe's carries "Simply Lite" chocolate bars in dark and milk chocolate flavors. They're great on their own, but because they're sweetened with maltitol, three squares are about all most of us can handle without gastric distress. They work well melted for frosting. Lily's Sugar-Free Chocolate Chips are great for cookies, or when you need something chocolate but don't want a commitment. They're stevia sweetened, but taste remarkably good in spite of that.

Sweeteners. See page 40. Go with monk fruit or chicory root, both of which are available in different grinds or styles online, and are used pretty much in the same measurements you would sugar. Experiment with the other ones, if you must, of course. But if you don't have the time or patience for that, use monk fruit and call it a day.

Truffle salt. So what if you've never eaten a truffle in your life! Order yourself some of this online, or pick it up next time you're in a gourmet kitchen store. You can buy black truffle salt or white truffle salt; either one is sublime. A few shakes, and the most ordinary pasta dish, the most inane little vegetable soup, is suddenly transformed into something amazing. It's a powerful scent and flavor, so just a bit goes a long way. Not everyone loves it. But if you do, (and boy, we do; some of us never go anywhere without it) it's culinary magic. You'll wind up using it in all kinds of things and wondering how you ever managed without it.

Truffle oil. When your truffle fix comes in oil, it needs to be kept cool and has a short shelf life. GREAT GIFT.

Unsweetened applesauce, canned. See note on canned crushed pineapple. Even better, make applesauce yourself and freeze it (page 82).

Vegenaise. You find it in the refrigerated departments of health food stores. Made without eggs, it tastes better, fresher, than conventional mayonnaise.

Vanilla extract. Most any kind will do the job. Buy gluten-free, just in case anybody's sensitive.

Vinegar. You'll want to have a basic apple cider vinegar, along with two or three good balsamic flavors. Try to buy where you can taste them before buying. My two current favorites are Sigona's Gravenstein Apple Balsamic and Sigona's Blenheim Apricot Balsamic.

Brownies and Other Breakfasts

The brownies and donuts that follow are magic in several ways. First, they're super cinchy to make. You pretty much throw everything in a bowl, mix it up, and bake it.

econd, they're packed with nutrition. They're actually a healthy little meal in a delightful, portable form factor. But, please, you have to remember not to say a thing to anybody until after they've eaten those spectacular brownies, donuts, and muffins. Most folks just can't imagine that anything healthy, nutritious, plant-based, or sugar-free can taste so decadent.

So, yes, eat these brownies (and donuts and pancakes) for breakfast, lunch, dinner, or when you just really need a brownie or a donut. Share them with your pals, kids. Just, please, keep the nutrition details to yourself, or save them for a post-treat surprise.

MIMI'S BADASS BROWNIES

These deeply, darkly chocolate, moist, and gooey things are sugar-free, gluten-free, *low in calories, low in carbs, and a good source of protein and fiber.* Not to mention vitamins, minerals, healthy fats. Made with egg replacer (see next page), they're also vegan.

This is a miracle. A brownie, ferpetesake: a fabulous, moist, frosted brownie, that has a better nutrition profile than nearly all of the "healthy" snack bars on grocery store shelves. Plus, you'll know exactly what's in them, and can pronounce all of it. They're basically made from a vegetable, plus nuts and cocoa beans.

But wait, there's more. Or, actually, less.

Figuring you spent $13 on ingredients ($7 almond butter (or twice that at fancier markets), $2 pumpkin, $1.50 eggs, or egg substitute, $2.50 for the rest), you've made 24 brownies for 54 cents a piece. *Helllooooooo.* And they're not some crummy snack bar, they're a REAL BROWNIE.

Wash a couple of these bad boys down with some great black coffee for breakfast. Pack some for lunch or the trail. Have one for dessert. Or skip dinner and go right for the brownies. Have two. They freeze well, too. (Yah, as if you're going to have any left to freeze.)

directions Blend ingredients by hand or electric mixer until smooth. Add sugar-free chocolate chips and/or walnuts if you want. Spread in a (8 x 8" or 9 x 13") baking dish greased with coconut oil. Bake at 350° for 20-35 minutes, until a toothpick comes out clean. The smaller pan takes a longer baking time.

Frosting: melt (nuke) 1 bar sugar-free dark chocolate just until soft—12-15 seconds—with 3 or 4 Tbsp. unsweetened soy or coconut milk. Stir well, until completely blended, and pour or spoon over brownies. If you frost while they're still warm, frosting will soak into the brownies a bit. Decorate with pecans or walnuts. When cooled, cover tightly and refrigerate. Brownies get even better after a day or two in the fridge, although it's kinda hard to wait. Cut into 24 glorious little squares.

ingredients

1 (16 oz.) jar creamy raw almond butter (roasted okay)

3 eggs or replacer

1 can or box pumpkin or butternut squash (about 2 cups) or less. Use half the amount if you want your brownies gooier: more for more cake texture.

1-1/2 cup granular or powdered sweetener

1 Tbsp. vanilla extract

1/2 cup unsweetened cocoa powder

1/2 tsp. salt

1 tsp. baking soda

1 tsp. cinnamon

Frosting:

1 bar (3.5 oz.) sugar-free dark chocolate (or equivalent amount of sugar-free semi-sweet chocolate chips)

4 Tbsp. unsweetened soy milk (or coconut milk, oat milk)

One 2-1/2" square frosted brownie with added nuts:

Calories 162
Total fat 10 g
Saturated fat .5 g
Sodium 114 mg
Potassium 463 mg
Total carbs 10 g
Fiber 5 g
Net carbs 5 g
Protein 8 g

59

Eggs/replacements

✳ Even though it says "substitute" or "egg replacer" for eggs, if you want to use eggs, use eggs! From happy, healthy, local chickens, of course, whose names you know, from neighbors or farmers whose names you know. Even more important than knowing their names, you should know what those hens have been eating. Grass, worms, weeds, disgusting little slugs? Perfect! That deep golden yolk tells you it's full of good stuff. Just keep in mind how many, and how much animal fat you're consuming. Yes, eggs count as "animal fat," but they're good food.

60

PASSERIFORMES: ICTERIDÆ.

PUMPKIN PIE SPICE DONUTS

We all secretly crave donuts, so why not make them yourself, without all that oil, sugar, and flour? Why not make insanely fabulous donuts that you can also feel virtuous for eating? These are donuts you can give to your kids and feel like parent-of-the-year. They're full of actual vitamins, minerals, protein, good fats. And, I promise you, they're divine.

Grab one of these puppies on your way out the door, and you're good to go. Give one to that sleepy kid who never wants breakfast as they climb into your school-bound SUV. These beauties won't spill in the car or on the subway.

You may be tempted, if you're eating them in public, to respond to the side-eye you'll get, with something like "I know, doesn't it look evil? But I'm diabetic, so I have to eat things like this."

It's fine to just use pumpkin pie spice (you stocked up in October, right?) in these donuts, but some folks prefer the "extra spicy" version with added nutmeg. There are no wrongs here. Imagine that! *Donuts with no wrongs.* A diabetic's dream come true.

directions Blend all ingredients until smooth with an electric mixer or by hand, then spoon or squeeze batter into a donut baking pan greased with coconut oil. Fill each donut form by about half. Bake at 350° for 15-20 minutes or until firm to the touch. Makes 12-14 donuts. No donut pan? No worries. Make muffins instead.

Let the pan cool for at least 20-30 minutes, then gently pry at the edges of each donut with a rounded, not sharp, knife, to loosen it, before lifting it out of the pan. You can also turn the pan over onto a tray, tap it gently, and release the donuts that way.

ingredients

16 oz. creamy raw almond butter (roasted almond butter okay)

2 eggs or replacer

1 cup canned pumpkin

1 cup powdered or granulated sweetener

1 Tbsp. vanilla extract

1/4 tsp. salt

1 tsp. baking soda

2 Tbsp. pumpkin pie spice

Coconut oil for greasing pan

One donut:

215 calories

Total fat 17 g

Saturated fat 2 g

Sodium 229 mg

Potassium 298 mg

Carbs 9 g

Fiber 4 g

Net carbs 5 g

Protein 7 g

Vinegar. Who knew?

Who even thinks about vinegar? We're talking about the plain old apple cider kind, made by mixing crushed apples and yeast, which ferments the sugars and turns them into alcohol. As more bacteria is added, the alcohol turns into acetic acid—the main active compound in vinegar. Organic, unfiltered apple cider vinegar also contains a substance called "mother," (creepy but true) made of proteins, enzymes, and friendly bacteria.

It's thought that "mother" is responsible for most of vinegar's health benefits, although it's hard to find any science behind that belief. Apple cider vinegar doesn't contain many vitamins or minerals, just a little potassium, some amino acids, and antioxidants.

It's been used for everything from cleaning and disinfecting, treating nail fungus, lice, warts, and ear infections, and as a food preservative, inhibiting bacteria like *E. coli* from growing in and spoiling food.

Recently, research suggests that vinegar can help with blood sugar and insulin levels. One small study suggests vinegar may improve insulin sensitivity by as much as 19–34% during a high carb meal and significantly lower blood sugar and insulin response.

Plus, for a measly three calories per tablespoon, apple cider vinegar may contribute to weight loss by promoting satiety, lowering blood sugar, and reducing insulin levels.

So, cook with it, add it to salads and soups, or dilute it with water and drink it. Then, when all this great research comes out to confirm the huge benefits vinegar offers, you can be very smug, and a bit healthier.

VINEGAR PUMPKIN SPICE DONUTS

This version, with the soda + vinegar hack, is a bit lighter and fluffier, but it takes two bowls, and a bit of precision in the timing. Worth it? Your call.

directions Mix ingredients in the big bowl with an electric mixer, if you have one, or thoroughly by hand. Combine baking soda and vinegar in the small bowl: it will bubble. Add to big bowl mixture and stir for 10 seconds. Squeeze or spoon into greased donut pan until each donut form is about half full, and bake at 350° for 12 minutes or until slightly firm to the touch. Makes 12 donuts or more.

Let the pan cool for at least 20-30 minutes, then gently pry at the edges of each donut with a rounded, not sharp, knife, to loosen it, before lifting it out of the pan. You can also turn the pan over onto a tray, tap it gently, and release the donuts that way.

Frost with Orange, Vanilla, Chocolate, or Maple Fondant Frosting, page 73.

ingredients

(Big Bowl)

1 cup pumpkin

2 eggs or replacer

12 oz. (1-1/2 cup) almond butter

1 cup sweetener (either "baking" or granulated grind)

1 tsp. vanilla

1 Tbsp. pumpkin pie spice (plus extra nutmeg if you want)

1/8 cup soy milk

(Small bowl)

2 tsp. baking soda

1/4 cup apple cider vinegar

Coconut oil for greasing pan

One donut:
Calories 216
Total fat 17 g
Saturated fat 2 g
Sodium 229 mg
Potassium 298 mg
Total carbs 9 g
Fiber 4 g
Net carbs 5 g
Protein 8 g

NOT-SO-RED VELVET DONUTS

Just the words "red velvet" are delicious, aren't they? Instead of calling them "light chocolate," "red velvet" is so much more cinematic. "Red velvet" says party. It says decadent, in a kind of 1950s way. But then there's the thing about how that red color got there. Red Dye #40. Which, although it's not going to kill anybody on contact, is made from petroleum, banned in the United Kingdom, and has been associated with health problems in children. That redness never added anything by the way of texture or taste to red velvet cakes or cupcakes, so howbout we just skip the "red" and keep the "velvet" idea and make ourselves a tender, gorgeous, chocolate donut.

directions Mix ingredients in the big bowl with an electric mixer, or thoroughly by hand.

Combine baking soda and vinegar in the small bowl: it will bubble. Add to big bowl mixture and stir for 10 seconds. Pour into greased donut pan and bake at 350° for 12 minutes or more, or until slightly firm to the touch. Makes 12 donuts.

Frost with Vanilla Frosting, page 72. Add a little cherry juice, from frozen cherries, if you want that pink color.

ingredients

(Big bowl)

1/4 cup coconut flour

2 cups almond flour

1/2 tsp. salt

1 tsp. vanilla

1 cup "buttermilk" (1 cup soy milk + 1 Tbsp. apple cider vinegar, let sit for a minute to thicken)

2 eggs or replacer

3/4 cup powdered sweetener

3 Tbsp. unsweetened cocoa powder

(Small bowl)

2 tsp. baking soda

1/4 cup apple cider vinegar

Coconut oil for greasing pan

One donut:

Calories 164

Total fat 11 g

Saturated fat 1 g

Sodium 250 mg

Potassium 206 mg

Total carbs 11 g

Fiber 3 g

Net carbs 8 g

Protein 6 g

Sugar-free sprinkles!

How cool is that? From Good Dees, at gooddees.com. Sweetened with erythritol and colored naturally. Not enough calories or carbs to worry about.

Let's compare ingredients, just for the heck of it.

Our Not-So-Red Velvet Donut

Coconut Flour

Almond Flour

Monk Fruit Sweetener

Soy Milk

Cocoa

Eggs

Vinegar

Baking Soda

Vanilla

Salt

Their Brand Name, Drive-Thru, Red Velvet Donut

Donut: (Enriched Wheat Flour (Wheat Flour, Niacin, Reduced Iron, Thiamine Mononitrate, Riboflavin, Folic Acid), Water, Palm Oil, Soybean Oil, Sugar. Contains 2% or Less of Each of the Following: Yeast, Soy Lecithin, Hydrogenated Soybean Oil, Mono- and Diglycerides, Salt, Wheat Gluten, Monocalcium Phosphate, Dried Milk Powder, Cellulose Gum, Lecithin, Maltodextrin, Calcium Propionate (To Maintain Freshness), Ascorbic Acid, Sorbitan Monostearate, Tocopherols, Enzymes, Oat Fiber, Egg Yolks. Filling: Sugar, Palm Oil, Water, Maltodextrin, Corn Syrup, Dextrose, Corn Starch, Salt, Mono And Diglycerides, Natural And Artificial Flavors (Milk), Mono and Diglycerides, Polysorbate 60, Soy Lecithin, Potassium Sorbate (To Maintain Freshness), Sodium Propionate (To Maintain Freshness), Phosphoric Acid, Yellow 5, Yellow 6, Citric Acid, Sodium Benzoate (To Maintain Freshness). Icing: Sugar, Water, Corn Syrup, Artificial Color, Natural Flavor, Agar, Potassium Sorbate (To Maintain Freshness), Citric Acid, Mono And Diglycerides, Locust Bean Gum, Salt. Icing: Sugar, Cream Cheese (Milk, Cream, Salt, Carob Bean Gum, Cheese Culture), Vegetable Shortening (Palm Oil, Canola Oil, Mono and Diglycerides, Polysorbate 60), Dextrose, Cream Cheese Powder (Cream Cheese Solids [Cream, Nonfat Milk, Salt, Sodium Alginate, Lactic Acid], Corn Syrup Solids, Sodium Caseinate [Milk], Natural Flavor), Corn Starch, Soybean Oil, Salt, Natural Flavor, Benzoic Acid (To Maintain Freshness), Polysorbate 60, Propyl Gallate, Colored with Beta Carotene. Filling: Sugar, Water, Palm Oil, Soybean Oil, Cocoa Powder (Processed with Alkali), Corn Syrup Solids, Soybean Oil, Palm Oil, Corn Starch, Salt, Mono and Diglycerides, Polysorbate 60, Natural and Artificial Flavors, Chocolate Liquor, Enzyme Modified Soy Protein, Sodium Caseinate (Milk), Sodium Hexametaphosphate, Soy Lecithin, Citric Acid, TBHQ). Nonpareils: Sugar, Corn Starch, Confectioner's Glaze, Yellow 5, Carnauba Wax, Red 3, Blue 1, Red 40, Yellow 6, Blue 2), Food Coloring (Water, High Fructose Corn Syrup, Glycerin, Red 40, Sugar, Modified Corn Starch, Red 3, Blue 1, Carrageenan, Maltodextrin, Dextrose, Potassium Sorbate (To Maintain Freshness), Xanthan Gum, Citric Acid). Confectionery Decoration: Sugar, Water, Egg White Powder, Modified Corn Starch, Cream of Tartar, Yellow 5, Water, Food Coloring, Water, High Fructose Corn Syrup, Glycerine, Yellow 5, Sugar, Modified Corn Starch, Blue 1, Carrageenan, Maltodextrin, Dextrose, Potassium Sorbate (To Maintain Freshness), Xanthan Gum, Citric Acid. 10/15/2020

SMASHING PUMPKIN CAKE & MUFFINS

Make a bunch. If you're gonna mess the kitchen up and get goo on your sweatshirt, make it worth your while.

These muffins are moist and fabulous even without frosting, and easier to carry with you. Freeze them in airtight container.

In cake form, perfect for an autumn birthday or celebration any time, even if you're just celebrating the fact that you can eat cake.

directions Throw muffin/cake ingredients into bowl and blend until smooth with electric mixer, or by hand. Spoon into two 8" round baking pans, well greased with coconut oil, or fill muffin papers in pan about 2/3 full.

No papers? Just grease each muffin space generously with coconut oil. They'll pop out with a little nudging with a butter knife when cool.

Bake at 350-375° for 20+ minutes until firm to the touch on top and a toothpick comes out clean. Cool before frosting.

Frost with Cream Cheese, Maple, Vanilla, Orange, or Chocolate Frosting.

One muffin:

Calories 157

Total fat 11g

Saturated fat 1g

Sodium 225 mg

Potassium 239 mg

Total carbs 9 g

Fiber 3 g

Net carbs 6 g

Protein 5 g

ingredients

1 cup creamy raw almond butter (roasted okay) (cashew butter, or mix of cashew and almond okay)

3 eggs or replacer

1/2 can canned pumpkin (about 1 cup)

1-1/4 cup sweetener (baking or granulated grind)

1 Tbsp. vanilla extract

1/2 tsp. salt (or less)

1 tsp. baking soda

1 Tbsp. pumpkin pie spice (or more)

Finely grated peel of one orange or tangerine (reserve 1 Tbsp. for frosting)

Juice of 1/2 orange or whole tangerine

MAPLE FONDANT FROSTING

We all love those amazing work-of-art wedding cakes, don't we? But then you notice nobody wants to actually eat the smooth perfection, or the ribbons and flowers. That's because they're made with commercial, shelf-stable, rolled fondant, which is nearly all sugar and hydrogenated oil, or, sometimes, cellulose gum. Eeeeew. That's not what we're talking about here. This is a recipe for frosting that looks and works a bit like the pro-level stuff, dries solid enough to not squish when you touch it, but is actually great tasting. Even better, it won't cause so much as a blip on your glucometer. Excellent for donuts or cakes, especially pumpkin spice or chocolate.

directions In a small saucepan, boil everything but the powdered sugar substitute. Remove the boiled mixture from stove and gradually add the powdered monk fruit (or your favorite sweetener) while whisking.

It should be thick enough to coat the back of a spoon. Too watery? Add 1 Tbsp. sweetener at a time. Too thick? Add 1 Tbsp. of water at a time. It can be stored in an airtight container in the fridge for a few days.

To use on your donuts, the frosting should be slightly warmer than body temperature and the consistency of thick cream. If you refrigerate it, just warm it up again and it'll go back to its creamy consistency.

ingredients

1/2 cup water

1/4 cup Lakanto maple syrup (or equivalent)

1/2 tsp. vanilla

1/8 tsp. salt

5-1/2 cups powdered sweetener

Whole recipe:

Calories 33

Total fat 0 g

Sodium 416 mg

Total carbs 8 g

Fiber 6 g

Net carbs 2 g

MORE FABULOUS FROSTINGS

Vanilla Frosting:
1 cup powdered sweetener
1 tsp. vanilla
Tiny pinch fine salt
2 Tbsp. or more soy milk
Stir well. Add more liquid or monk fruit to make it thinner or thicker.

Maple Glaze:
1 cup powdered sweetener
1 tsp. vanilla
Tiny pinch fine salt
1 Tbsp. or more soy milk
1 Tbsp. Lakanto or equivalent maple syrup
Stir well. Add more liquid or monk fruit to make it thinner or thicker.

Whole recipe
Vanilla
or
Maple Glaze
Frosting:

Calories 25

Total fat, fiber, protein 0

Sodium 158 mg

Net carbs 2 g

Orange Frosting:

Blend juice of one orange, 1/2 tsp. vanilla, and add powdered sweetener until you get the thickness you want. Start with 1/2 cup. Drizzle over donuts with a spoon or squeeze bottle, and decorate with finely grated orange rind.

Whole recipe:

Calories 89	Fiber 0 g
Total fat 0 g	Net carbs 20 g
Potassium 318 mg	Protein 1 g
Carbs 20 g	

Cream Cheese Frosting:

To 16 oz. vegan cream cheese, add 1/2 cup powdered sweetener, 1 Tbsp. grated orange peel, 1/2 tsp. vanilla; thin slightly with soy or coconut milk. Stir until blended.

Whole recipe:

Calories 833	Carbs 35 g
Total fat 98 g	Fiber 17 g
Sodium 2434 g	Net carbs 18 g
Potassium 53 mg	Protein 34 g

Chocolate Frosting:

Put four squares of Trader Joe's Simply Lite Sugar-Free Chocolate (or an equivalent amount of Lily's sugar-free chips) in a microwave-safe dish with 2 Tbsp. soy or coconut milk. Nuke for just a short burst—10 or 15 seconds—until the milk starts to bubble. Remove from the microwave and stir until the chocolate is melted, then drizzle over cooled donuts.

Whole recipe:

Calories 310	Carbs 61 g
Total fat 25 g	Fiber 12 g
Saturated fat 15 g	Net carbs 5 g
Sodium 9 mg	Protein 5 g
Potassium 598 mg	

Another Chocolate Frosting:

1 cup powdered sweetener
3 Tbsp. cocoa powder
2 Tbsp. soy milk
1 tsp. vanilla
Stir and frost.

Whole recipe:

Calories 77	Total carbs 7 g
Total fat 4 g	Fiber 4 g
Saturated fat 15 g	Net carbs 3 g
Sodium 4 mg	Protein 4 g
Potassium 41 mg	

MISS H'S PUMPKIN PANCAKES

Pancakes are the golden retriever of foods. They have no bite; just loving, comforting sweetness. They're familiar and warm, but with character. No wonder they're the first dish lots of kids learn to make on the stove. These are called "Miss H's" because they are my granddaughter, Helen's, favorite, and the first thing she learned to cook.

Pancakes are the perfect way to slide yourself, your family, your partner, your pals into a healthier way of eating with no offensive edges. A great gateway food. Nothing obviously green or full of fiber. Pancakes! What could possibly be creepy or clinical about pancakes? If you're feeding folks who turn their snoots up at the hint of anything extra healthy with "artificial sweeteners" in it, start here.

Plus, although they're up here in the front with the breakfasts, why not have these for dinner, with a veggie-packed smoothie on the side? Oh, yeah.

directions Whisk everything but the dry mix together until it's smooth, then add the pancake mix, not all at once, just until it makes the batter thick enough but not gluey or gummy. It should be liquid enough to easily spread out in the pan. Add more coconut milk if it's too thick. Don't stir it any more than you have to: don't bruise the batter! Just move it around enough to get all the dry ingredients wet, but don't try to get rid of all the bumps and lumps.

Get a griddle or frying pan hot, but not smoking, and add a blop or two of coconut oil to the pan. Watch the heat—keep it in the medium range. Cook those puppies! Keep enough coconut oil in the pan to make the edges of the pancakes crispy.

Garnish with fresh fruit—black or blueberries or strawberries are beautiful on these—with one of the good sugar-free maple syrup substitutes.

ingredients

6 oz. organic canned pumpkin (1/2 of 12-oz. can)

1 egg or replacer

1 tsp. vanilla

Juice of 1 whole orange, plus plenty of grated rind

1 Tbsp., heaping, pumpkin pie spice (or more)

1/3 cup soy milk

Dash of salt (tiny bit!)

1 tsp. sweetener

1 cup whole grain pancake mix. (Bob's Red Mill, Trader Joe's... buckwheat, whole grain, or gluten-free.)

4 pancakes (recipe makes about 16)

Calories 132

Total fat 2 g

Sodium 234 mg

Total carbs 25 g

Fiber 4 g

Net carbs 21 g

Protein 5 g

Pumpkins, I love you.

You're the color of sunshine and marigolds and poppies. You last for weeks with no refrigeration, and look fabulous as kitchen decor, just sitting around waiting to be eaten. Not only is your sweet meat delicious, but you are full of seeds! Two entirely different foods, shapes, colors, textures, in one gorgeous golden package. No wonder you have not one, but two, of your own holidays.

Also, dear Pumpkin, you are **a perfect, nutritious replacement for fat and flour, and you're a vegetable.** Full of vitamins, fiber, great texture.

If you want that pumpkin taste, it's there; if you don't want to taste pumpkin, you hide it with chocolate or orange or peppers.

With a good supply of canned pumpkin in the larder, a person is set, in so many ways. Yes, canned food is "processed" food. But there's nothing but pumpkin in that can, and it's a way better choice than the flour, sugar, oil, and butter it's replacing. You can also buy it in a box.

They're easy to grow, too, if you have a little space, and they're particularly fond of compost heaps. Choose a sugar pie variety for great taste. Plus, bonus points for efficiency. You'll notice a number of the recipes in this book are made from the same ingredients, and that those ingredients—like pumpkin—are easy to find, easy to store, and will keep well, for the most part. If you already have the ingredients on hand, **you don't have to wander out at odd hours** to find what you need when you're hit with an overwhelming donut urge.

Don't be like my bff, D, who threw her trench coat on over her undies one night, late, and headed out for the Ralph's market down the street from where we lived in North Hollywood. It was about 1970; D was an aspiring actress; I aspired to having the cash for groceries. We were baking, we needed butter, and it wouldn't wait. She jumped in her awful old pale blue VW and headed out. As she told the story, when she got back, she had been leaning over the dairy case, muttering, looking for the unsalted butter, per my request. As she sorted through the margarines and yogurts, she heard an oddly familiar male voice next to her, also in search of something in the dairy case. She froze with recognition, trying to turn just enough to confirm her suspicion without being seen herself, in her 10 p.m., no-makeup, bad-hair state. Yes, it was Charles Bronson, in search of ice cream. She turned the other way and left, fast, without the unsalted butter.

For you young'uns who may not remember Bronson, it was like bumping into Brad Pitt in the frozen foods aisle. Not that a Brad Pitt or Charles Bronson particularly cares, but you just don't want to arrive at that moment, in bad undies with no lip gloss, *because you didn't stock up.*

REAL TOAST

A recipe for toast? Really? Yup. If you make toast this way, you can make it for a whole bunch of hungry people at once. Try that in a two-slot toaster. Plus, when you make it this way, it tastes better. There are only two ingredients, so be sure to get them both right.

The bread should be a really good sourdough, which means it's fermented, which means it's a good thing to put in your body. The bread will only have a couple of ingredients: whole grain flour, which can be real wheat or rye or some other type of grain; water; maybe a bit of salt. My favorite bakery, Companion Bakeshop in Santa Cruz, makes bread like this from locally grown grains just like your great-grandma ate. Sometimes they put walnuts or cranberries in the bread, which grownups love, but kids aren't so crazy about.

The second ingredient, vegan butter, is almost entirely pure fat, but it's not animal fat. WayFare is an excellent brand—made from butter beans! —and there are others you may find you like better than "real" butter.

directions Cut the bread in whatever size pieces you want. Triangles or semi-circles look good on a plate, and they're an easy size to bite without getting goo all over your face. Spread a small amount of vegan butter on each piece. Put them all on a cookie sheet or pizza pan. Bake in a 400° oven for about 10 minutes, or until they're as done as you like.

Cinnamon toast? Sure. Sprinkle cinnamon and granulated sweetener. There ya go. Avocado toast? Next page!

ingredients

Good sourdough bread
Vegan butter

1 oz. piece walnut sourdough:

Calories 70

Total fat .5 g

Sodium 90 mg

Potassium 56 mg

Total carbs 9.5 g

Fiber 1 g

Net carbs 8.5 g

Protein 2.5 g

1 Tbsp. vegan butter:

Calories 90

Total fat 10 g

Saturated fat 8 g

Sodium 65 mg

Walnut sourdough from Acme Bread in Berkeley, CA. Real bread baked and sold by earnest young folks who are really into it.

AVOCADO TOAST

Yes, it's trendy. It's also fast and easy to make with things you already have, or will have, once you've digested this book. It's absolutely delicious; addictively so. It's super nutritious. And—my favorite—it's so beautiful.

directions Start with good bread. Really good bread. Sourdough, whole grain, maybe with some walnuts or olives in it. Toast it. Squish some avocado on it. Add a squeeze of lemon, and depending upon what else you have at the bottom of your crisper, a few slices of radish, sliced very thin; some chopped arugula, basil, or Italian parsley and sliced fresh tiny tomatoes if you can get 'em. Sprinkle with your favorite salt or seed mix. I like Trader Joe's "Everything but the Bagel," or smoky salt.

If you've got more than one guest, put it all on the table in pretty dishes for them to assemble themselves.

ingredients

Bread

Avocado

Lemon

Arugula (optional)

Radishes (optional)

Basil (optional)

Parsley (optional)

Microgreens (optional)

Tiny tomatoes (optional)

Smoky, truffle, or "bagel" salt (optional)

SAUTÉED APPLES

Get good apples from a farmer's market if you can, or a neighbor with a tree, or somewhere you can be sure they haven't been sprayed with pesticide or dipped in wax. This is a great way to use up sad, beat-up apples that have been in the fridge too long, The important thing is that they are apples that start out tasting really good. A little tart, maybe: an apple with character.

directions Cut off any yucky parts of the apples. Leave the skin if it's not too beat up. Slice the apple into quarters, remove the core, then cut into small, thin slices.

Heat a couple of teaspoons of coconut oil or vegan butter in a frying pan, then add the apple slices. Squeeze fresh lemon juice onto the slices: at least a half a lemon's worth of juice, and a whole lemon if you're cooking three or four apples. Sensitive to citrus? Just leave out the lemon, and the apples will still taste lovely.

Stir and cook the apple slices until they're soft. Add a spoonful or two of cinnamon and some sweetener.

Serve them with pancakes, french toast, vegan ice cream, or all by themselves.

ingredients

5-6 apples

Lemon juice (one lemon for 5-6 apples)

Vegan butter (2 tsp. for 5-6 apples)

1 Tbsp. or more cinnamon

APPLESAUCE

Applesauce makes a great substitute for oil in baking recipes: out goes the fat and in goes lovely fragrance and subtle apple flavor. It's also a great snack, good topping for pancakes, and excellent all-around side dish. Plus, huge benefit: it makes your home smell fantastic while it's cooking. Make a bunch and freeze some, remembering to leave room in the jars so they don't burst when they freeze.

With crisp, slightly tart apples from your own or your neighbor's trees, or the farmer's market, ordinary applesauce becomes amazing. Leaving the peel on, in addition to saving time and your fingers, adds color and fiber.

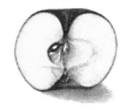

directions Same as sautéed apples, page 81, except cut the apples up in smaller pieces, and skip the vegan butter. Put about a half inch of water in the pan, then add the lemon. The lemon keeps the apples from oxidizing and turning brown, plus adds an acid hit for better flavor. Add cinnamon and apples; cook, covered, 10 minutes or more until the apples are tender. Squish them up a bit if they need it, but leave it a little lumpy so it looks authentic. If you prefer your applesauce smoother, run it through a food processor for a few pulses, or squish it enthusiastically with your potato masher. Don't cook it forever hoping to cook out the lumps.

ingredients

5-6 apples

Lemon juice (one lemon for 5-6 apples)

Cinnamon (1 Tbsp. or more)

1/6 whole recipe:

Calories 112

Total fat 0 g

Saturated fat 0 g

Sodium 2 mg

Potassium 258 mg

Total carbs 28 g

Fiber 6 g

Net carbs 22 g

Protein 1g

STEWED APRICOTS

You can use either dried or fresh apricots. If your apricots are yummy, fresh, sweet ones (my favorite are Blenheims), don't cook 'em, eat 'em! Nothing more divine than a really great apricot. Trouble is, most apricots these days aren't that good. They might be big and orange and look just fine, but that doesn't mean they taste good. Some of the best apricots in the world are small and a bit sorry looking.

If what you have are dried apricots or not-great fresh ones, here's how to make them fabulous.

directions Put sliced fresh apricots or dried apricots halves in a pot with a little water—enough to make about an inch of water in the bottom of the pan. Bring the water to a boil, then turn it down to a simmer, put the lid on, and cook for 15 or 20 minutes. When they're soft, pour off most of the excess water; leave a little water. Add the juice of 1/2 to 1 whole lemon and a few spoonfuls of sugar-like substance if you want more sweetness, and sprinkle with cinnamon.

If you want the liquid to be thicker, more like jam, add a spoonful of psyllium. What the heck is psyllium? See page 54.

The longer they sit in the lemony, cinnamony liquid, the better they get. Put them in the fridge and use them with pancakes or vanilla cake, page 170, or just eat them. Heaven.

ingredients

Apricots

Sweetener

A lemon

Cinnamon

Psyllium (optional)

1 cup sliced:
Calories 80
Total fat .6 g
Saturated fat 0 g
Sodium 2 mg
Potassium 427 mg
Total carbs 18 g
Fiber 3.3 g
Net carbs 14.7 g
Protein 2.3 g

got too much sugar in some form or and they don't
belong. For example, raisins. I hate 'em.

Customize this with your favorite nuts, or maybe some coconut, but
here are the basics.

directions: Preheat oven to 325°. Put the dry ingredients in a big
bowl, stir it up, then add the coconut oil and maple syrup and mix that up.
Spread it on a big baking sheet, about 17 x 12", with sides so it doesn't spill.

Bake until the granola starts to brown, maybe 25 minutes. Stir it with a
spatula and keep cooking until it's light golden brown, which might take
another 15 or 20 minutes. Don't let it burn!

When you take it out of the oven, mix in the dried fruit. Store it in an
airtight container at room temperature or in the freezer. Makes 12-16 or more
generous servings.

ingredients:
4-1/2 cups old-fashioned rolled oats
3/4 cup raw sunflower seeds
1-1/2 cups coarsely chopped raw almonds
2 Tbsp ground cinnamon
1 cup Lakanto maple syrup or equivalent
1/3 cup melted coconut oil
1 cup dried apricots or dried cranberries

1/12 recipe, 1 large serving, apricot version
Calories 336
Total fat 21 g
Sodium 41 mg
Potassium 117 mg
Total carbohydrates 32 g
Dietary fiber 6 g
Net carbohydrates 26 g
Protein 9 g

28

WORLD'S GREATEST GRANOLA

Wander the grocery store or "health food" aisles all you want: you won't see a packaged granola that's as fabulous as this. They've all either got too much sugar in some form or another, or ingredients that just don't belong. For example, raisins. I hate 'em.

Customize this with your favorite nuts, or maybe some coconut, but here are the basics.

directions Preheat oven to 325°. Put dry ingredients in a big bowl, stir them up, then add the coconut oil and maple syrup and mix that up. Spread it on a big baking sheet, about 17 x 12", with sides so it doesn't spill.

Bake until the granola starts to brown, maybe 25 minutes. Stir it with a spatula and keep cooking until it's light golden brown, which might take another 15 or 20 minutes. Don't let it burn!

When you take it out of the oven, mix in the dried fruit. Store it in an airtight container at room temperature or in the freezer. Makes 12-16 or more generous servings.

1/12 recipe: 1 large serving, apricot version:

Calories 336

Total fat 21 g

Sodium 41 mg

Potassium 117 mg

Total carbs 32 g

Fiber 6 g

Net carbs 26 g

ingredients

4-1/2 cups old-fashioned rolled oats

3/4 cup raw sunflower seeds

1-1/2 cups coarsely chopped raw almonds

2 Tbsp. ground cinnamon

1 cup Lakanto maple syrup or equivalent

1/3 cup melted coconut oil

1 cup dried apricots or dried cranberries

Save-the-Day Soups

If you're looking to control your weight, manage your blood glucose, improve your digestion and energy, soup is your new best pal. Wait, not salad? If you like salad, great; just watch those dressings, and know that some people have trouble digesting raw vegetables.

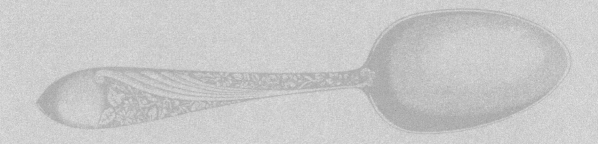

Plus, with soup, you get extra benefits. Because you can't easily eat soup in the car, or standing at the sink, it's a civilizing influence, and helps you get your water in, as well as four or five veggies in one bowl. And it makes you feel full. Salad? Not so much. Don't get me wrong. Love salad. Huge salad fan. But soup! Sometimes you really need warmth.

In fact, **soup is about the only practical way to get all the nutrition you need into your life.** You do some work up front, and reap the rewards for days or weeks. Make that big batch of soup, put individual servings in jars to take to work or school. A thermos works, too, but there's something nice about a clear mason jar full of gorgeous red pepper soup that you warm up in the microwave. Freeze a bunch of soup in jars, remembering to leave room for the freezing liquid to expand. Then, for six months or so, you open the freezer, grab that jar, and off you go. Still frozen? Not defrosted? That's okay, so long as you have access to a way to heat it up.

Soup lasts, it's portable, it travels well, it's flexible—sauces, casseroles, all kinds of things—and as long as you're making it with whole foods, mostly plants, and not adding a bunch of oil, you're eating beautifully. And don't let anybody shame you about "too many peas—carbs!" or "watch out for all the sugar in those carrots!" Please. You don't have a carrot problem. Or a pea problem. They're great food, and make great soups.

Please remember to **USE BLENDER CAUTION** when blending hot soups. Here's your special exploding blender icon, to remind you that when you blend hot soup, keep that lid on tight, or split the batches so the blender isn't too full of hot stuff. This reminder is from an abundance of caution, of course. You may be way more sensible than certain cookbook-writing grandmas who have, more than once, worn a large serving of hot goo on the front of their shirt.

91

GENIUS SOUP, AGAIN

Since I first published this recipe years ago, I've heard from so many people who've made it a habit, which is exactly what food geeks like me live for. So here is Genius Soup, again, because I *want* you to make it a habit.

You will devote maybe half an hour of chopping and washing vegetables, and reap the rewards for a week or two afterwards. Or, freeze some, and pull it out months later.

Good soup feels good going down, and feels good after it's gone down, like you've really eaten something that matters. You *have* eaten something that matters.

directions Sauté celery, onion, garlic, and carrots in a tablespoon or more of water (or oil) in the bottom of a heavy stockpot until the onions are transparent. Add the broth, as much as you want, to fill up the pot about halfway or more. Add a quart or two of water. Dump in the tomatoes, all the chopped greens, salt, pepper, and cook it for at least two hours, way more is fine, adding more water or broth if it cooks down quite a bit.

Day one: When you serve it, sprinkle lots of chopped fresh parsley or cilantro on top, season it with salt and pepper and a generous squeeze or two of fresh lemon juice in each bowl.

Day two: Toss some brown rice noodles in with a potful of the soup. Bring it to a boil, then turn the flame off and leave covered until the noodles are cooked. Throw some canned cannellini beans in it to warm up. Add lemon and parsley on top. It's a whole, complete, lovely meal in a bowl, which you have prepared in seconds, practically, without harming one tiny bit of Styrofoam in the process. *Genius.*

No nutrition facts for Genius Soup? Nope. Too exhausting to list all the vitamins, minerals, fiber. Maybe some fat in the olive oil, divided by 20 or 30 servings. Basically all good, no bad.

ingredients

1 cup or more chopped celery (3-5 stalks)

1 or two onions

1 clove garlic (optional)

4 or 5 medium carrots or more small carrots

Olive oil (optional)

Vegetable broth

Canned, fresh, boxed, or frozen crushed or chopped tomatoes; 2 large cans or several large tomatoes or a quart or so cherry tomatoes

Chopped cabbage, spinach, chard, kale, arugula, collard greens, dandelions, in any combination, as much as you can stuff in the pot.

Fresh parsley or cilantro, lemon, salt and pepper

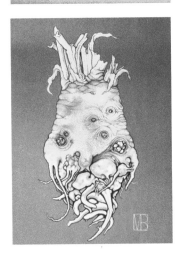

Day three: Throw some good salsa verde into bowls of the soup, and float a whole-grain tortilla or corn chips with grated cheese substitute and/or nutritional yeast flakes in there. Tortilla soup!

Day four: Put a piece of fresh fish in a shallow pan, cover it with Genius Soup and a generous squeeze of lemon or lime, heat it with a lid on until the fish flakes.

Of course, you can just keep riffing on it, too, and come up with your own personal variations. How about tossing a small bag of either cooked lentils or dried lentils, and cooking according to directions using your incredible soup base as the liquid? (See French-as-Hell Cassoulet on page 126.)

The other "genius" of this soup is that different family members can dress it differently—hot salsa on yours and some noodles and cheese in the kids'. Recalcitrant husbands can add meatballs to theirs. But you don't have to make multiple meals to begin your healthy eating journey.

We must warn you at this point, however, that you don't serve things like this to people you are casually dating and not at all serious about. Folks have been searching for centuries for potions and aphrodisiacs, when all they needed to do was make a really good pot of soup for the target of their adoration. Just, please, use it responsibly.

SPINACH SOUP & CREAMED SPINACH

When you sit down at a steak house—not that we're suggesting you do, but IF you do—scan the sides. Sure enough, there it is: creamed spinach, a small bowl, for $8, $10, maybe $12 bucks. Fuggedaboudit! Here's a better-tasting version that will help you amortize whatever you spent on this book. By making your own creamed spinach two or three times, you've recouped your investment completely, saved your guts from all that cream and butter, and given yourself several lovely doses of dark greens.

Make it with a cup or more of broth, and it's soup. Use less liquid, and you have creamed spinach without all the calories and excess sodium. Use it on top of toast for breakfast, on pasta, or under the Simple Salmon on page 152.

directions Nuke the spinach in the broth (or cook it in a pot on the stove) until tender, which is pretty much just until it's hot, and blend it in the blender or food processor with remaining ingredients. Keep your hand on the lid! Season to taste. Makes two generous servings. Blend the hot soup with an immersion blender, or VERY CAREFULLY in an upright blender—half at a time, so it doesn't blow hot soup all over.

1/2 recipe (with vegan feta and 1 Tbsp. vegan butter:	
Calories 198	
Total fat 11 g	
Sodium 1606 mg	
Potassium 946 mg	
Total carbs 11 g	
Fiber 4 g	
Net carbs 7 g	
Protein 14	

ingredients

A big bag or bunch of fresh spinach or a 10 oz. package of frozen spinach

1 cup or more vegetable broth

2 oz. vegan feta cheese or vegan cream cheese

Soy milk, coconut milk, as much as you want to make it creamier

1-2 Tbsp. of vegan butter (optional)

Salt

Pepper (lemon pepper is great here)

Nutmeg—just a sprinkle, then add to taste

MUSHROOM SOUP

It feels like a high in your belly, warm and smooth and simple and complex all at once. It's not photogenic, but performs like a pro as sauce, or gravy, in casseroles, or frozen for another day if you have any left over. Which you probably won't. Plus, it's all vegetables, with a little oil.

I gave this recipe to a lawyer I had retained once that I didn't know well. He got in touch with me weeks later to tell me that I should have warned him. He lived alone in Yreka, California, and didn't do a lot of cooking. Something made him decide to try this; I'm thinking he already had the mushrooms, and some bourbon, and gave it a go. What he told me was that he couldn't stop eating it, and ate the whole dang batch in one sitting. **He wasn't mad**; he just wanted me to know that I should have told him how good it was, and that he wouldn't be able to stop eating it. So consider yourself warned.

directions In a 2-quart or bigger saucepan with a lid, sauté the onion in half the oil/butter. When the onion starts to go transparent, add the mushrooms and the other half of the oil and/or butter and continue to saute for 6-8 minutes. Add the stock and most of the parsley; save a little to chop and garnish with. Simmer, covered, for an hour.

Add the sherry or bourbon. Blend the hot soup with an immersion blender, or VERY CAREFULLY in an upright blender—half at a time, so it doesn't blow hot soup all over. Season with salt and pepper. Makes four generous servings. Sharing encouraged.

One serving:

Calories 271

Total fat 20.5 g

Saturated fat 3 g

Sodium 228 mg

Potassium 777 mg

Total carbs 13.5 g

Fiber 2 g

Net carbs 10.5 g

Protein 3.5 g

ingredients

6 Tbsp. olive oil or vegan butter

1 sliced onion

12-16 oz. whole fresh mushrooms, whatever kind you like, (crimini and shiitake are great) or sliced white ones, if that's what you have, or a mix

4 cups (32 oz.) organic vegetable stock

A fistful of fresh parsley, preferably Italian, from the pot on your sink

2 oz. sherry or bourbon (not your best stuff: any bourbon will do) or apple cider vinegar if teetotaler

Truffle salt, pepper

Optional: vegan yogurt and tarragon for seasoning or garnish

CAULIFLOWER SOUP/SAUCE/MASH

Give it a chance, and cauliflower, this quiet beauty, this lovely, pale, round, modest, and soft-spoken jewel of the garden, will wind up being one of your favorites. Like a perfect best friend, it's there when you need it. It holds up. Even after a week or two in the fridge, starting to look a bit brownish on the edges, just trim off the brownish parts and cook the rest. Great raw, grilled, sautéed, but maybe most brilliant of all as soup.

Use less liquid in this recipe, and you have a side dish to use instead of mashed potatoes, that actually tastes better than most mashed potatoes. Use more liquid, and you've got a great little soup or vastly improved "white sauce" to use in mac'n'cheese and elsewhere. Sprinkle some turmeric or paprika on top for color and even more nutrition, or some chopped parsley or arugula on top, and/or add a nasturtium or two.

directions Nuke the cauliflower in the broth (or cook it in a pot on the stove) until it's tender, blend in the blender with remaining ingredients and season to taste.

When you blend it, keep going until it's smooth, unless you want it more potato-like and a bit lumpy. If you keep blending, it will develop a gorgeous, silky texture.

Whole recipe (2 large or 4 small servings):

Calories 288

Total fat 18 g

Saturated fat 8 g

Sodium 2138 mg

Potassium 16 mg

Total carbs 13 g

Fiber 12 g

Net carbs 1 g

Protein 15 g

ingredients

1 fresh head of cauliflower, cut up

1 cup or more vegetable broth

2 or 3 oz. vegan feta cheese

2 Tbsp. vegan butter or olive oil

Salt and pepper (lemon pepper works great here)

Nutmeg—just a sprinkle, then add to taste

Turmeric—for color

RED PEPPER SOUP

You are attracted to this brilliant orange for a reason. It signals, like other bright, beautiful food colors, nutrition. Or maybe it's more accurate to say, it *screams* nutrition.

Red Pepper Soup is beyond beautiful to look at, extremely easy to make, keeps well, is ready in 15 or 20 minutes. It can be a whole meal, with nutritional yeast flakes added, or a sauce for pasta, eggs, or fish. All that wonderful color also works as a great way to disguise other veggies that might be getting a bit tired in the crisper.

This soup also freezes well, so you'll have it when you need it: don't forget to leave room in the jar for the soup to expand when it freezes.

directions Cook the vegetables in the broth until tender, then blend in the blender (watch out, if it's hot!) with remaining ingredients and season to taste. Garnish with nutritional yeast flakes, chopped parsley, chives, nasturtiums, basil seeds, and leaves or microgreens.

Whole recipe:

Calories 150

Total fat 1 g

Sodium 395 mg

Potassium 525 mg

Total carbs 32 g

Fiber 8 g

Net carbs 24 g

Protein 5 g

ingredients

1 onion

3 big red or orange peppers cut in chunks

1 clove garlic (optional)

1 cup or more vegetable broth

Some carrots or zucchini if you want, or cabbage

Vegan feta cheese if you want (or whatever cheese you've got)

Salt (smoky salt or truffle salt)

BY-GUESS-AND-BY-GOLLY GAZPACHO

You may have met gazpacho as a snooty first course, served in tiny little cups on silver trays. Or, seasonally, on the appetizer menus in trendy bars and bistros.

Well, guess what. It's easy and fast to make, forgiving and beautiful. Put it in a pretty dish, throw a nasturtium blossom or two on top, and wow the heck out of your unsuspecting dinner guests. Or make a batch for yourself and put your face in it.

The time to make it is in the peak of summer, into fall, when the tomatoes and cucumbers are ripe. Try to find local, dry-farmed, organic tomatoes, or better yet, grow 'em yourself, in pots.

I have a friend who said she hated tomatoes. As she left my front yard one day, I demanded (trying hard not to be judgmental) that she pick a gorgeous, bright orange Sun Gold tomato from the raised bed and eat it, right then and there. She did. Instant convert.

If you're just starting with homegrown tomatoes, I highly recommend the teeny ones, "cherry" tomatoes like Sun Gold or Sweet 100s. Easy to grow, don't need structures, best taste of just about any tomato.

In a perfect world, you're growing the tomatoes, and the cucumbers, also a cinch to grow, and you just toss them in the blender with salsa, lime, and a pinch of salt. I prefer salsa verde, but a mild red salsa works fine, too.

directions Throw it all in a blender and blend until kinda, but not completely, smooth. Serve cold or at room temperature. Garnish with cilantro, edible flowers, or microgreens.

ingredients

A bunch of really good, really ripe chopped tomatoes, (or whole, if tiny) grown by actual people

A couple of cucumbers, peeled and cut into chunks

1/2 jar salsa verde (or red salsa, if that's what you have)

Juice of 1 lemon, lime or good vinegar

Dash of kosher flake salt

Serve with fancy salts

CARROT SOUP

You can go into any number of chi-chi restaurants and order a version of this for 8 or 10 bucks. Or you can just make it yourself in about 10 minutes and feel completely virtuous about the whole thing.

Remember to store your carrots separately from other fruits and vegetables so they don't get bitter. (Only certain fruits and veggies actually make carrots bitter, but who can remember which ones?)

 *directions* Nuke the vegetables in the broth (or cook them in a pot on the stove) until they're tender. Blend in the blender (hold that lid on!) or immersion blender with remaining ingredients and season to taste. Garnish with a sprinkle of nutritional yeast, freshly chopped parsley, or edible flowers, or all of that, on top.

Whole recipe:

Calories 287

Total fat 11 g

Saturated fat 2 g

Sodium 631 mg

Potassium 525 mg

Total carbs 32 g

Fiber 8 g

Net carbs 24 g

Protein 5 g

ingredients

4-5 big carrots, cut in chunks, or a bag of those little already-peeled babies

1 cup or more vegetable broth

1 garlic clove

An onion

If you're trying to use up that zucchini squash the neighbors gave you, throw that in, too

Salt

1-2 tsp. olive oil or vegan butter

PESTO

If you only get one new habit from this book, make it pesto. Or maybe brownies and pesto. Or, okay, brownies, donuts, and pesto. And Genius Soup. And pesto. It's here in the soup section because it's a brilliant way to doll up an everyday soup.

So much fabulous in one gooey green blop! Not only does it smell and taste like a celebration of earthly delights, it's a way to put leafy dark greens in your body at literally every meal. On a sandwich or avocado toast. Oh, yah. With beans or pasta or soup? Now you're talking. And when you make it yourself, with good, fresh, organic ingredients, it's worth doing just for the fragrance in your kitchen. It will last in the fridge for a few days, or can be frozen in cube trays so you can pop out a cube whenever you want.

When you make it yourself, you'll see with your own doubting eyes just how many leaves it takes to make one small jar. Which, I'm hoping, will make you realize how much crazy green power nutrition is packed in every spoonful.

Most people associate basil with pesto, and that's also delicious and fragrant, but more expected. Experiment using what you have in the garden (or your neighbor's or your mom's) or from the farmer's market. In addition to the greens listed in this recipe, kale, basil, spinach, dandelion greens, nasturtium leaves all make great pesto.

Leave out the garlic, and the pesto is still great. Use pine nuts instead of the other nuts if you want, but be sure you're getting actual pine nuts. Read the package carefully.

You can also buy pretty decent pesto in jars on the shelves and in the deli cases of better grocery stores, which we highly recommend as a backup.

directions Use a food processor: small is fine. Start with the nuts, nutritional yeast, and oil, then add the rest of the ingredients. Take the tougher stems off before you process the greens. Process until well blended, but not totally creamy.

ingredients

1 bunch cilantro (optional: some of us love it, some don't)

1 bunch arugula

1 bunch Italian parsley

1 bunch carrot tops

7 big garlic cloves

Grated peel of 2 lemons

Juice of 1-1/2 lemons

1 cup olive oil

1/2 cup sprouted almonds or raw almonds, cashews (slightly toasted is best), or pine nuts

1/2 cup nutritional yeast

Sea salt or kosher salt to taste

1/4 cup

Calories 260

Total fat 26 g

Saturated fat 2.5 g

Sodium 450 mg

Potassium 525 mg

Total carbs 3 g

Fiber 1 g

Net carbs 2 g

Protein 3 g

Things I learned in the garden.

Plant seeds everywhere. Some will come up. You never know which ones. Just keep planting seeds.

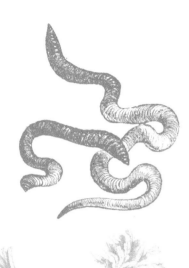

Keep at it. Pick a corner, weed, and dig.

Your best tools are your eyes, nose, and fingertips.

Walk around. Look.

You work and work and then, suddenly, there are miracles. Which are never really sudden, are they?

The more you have your hands in it, the more you realize it's not you at all.

Wiggle whenever you can. It's good for you. Let the worms be your teachers.

Your chard doesn't care if you think your thumbs are green or not.

Some things just won't grow in that spot, no matter what you do. Try something else.

When something pops up and looks interesting, don't kill it just because it wasn't in your plan. Sometimes the results you don't plan and weren't looking for are the most wonderful of all.

Don't expect bean plants to sprout tomatoes.

Most of the work of growing your plants is being done by creatures in the dirt you can't see. Be good to them.

Opposite page: "Watermelon" radishes from the farmer's market, served up with a slice of lemon. Could anything be more gorgeous? Also crunchy, delicious, and you could eat a bucket of them without gaining an ounce or causing even a slight blood sugar blip.

Cooking for Company

Born in 1946, I was part of a generation of women who were brought up to be homemakers. The art history, the nuclear physics, the medieval musicology was all fine, so long as we understood that we would spend the greatest part of our lives putting meals on tables and driving people other than ourselves to school. So I cooked.

nlike today, when celebrity chefs and TV cooking shows are all over the place, in the '60s, there was nothing chic about it. But in my late teens and early 20s, I found out that cooking wasn't something a lot of young folks my age did particularly well. Because I loved to eat, had limited to no funds, and liked jolly company, it was a way to keep my apartment on Coldwater Canyon Avenue buzzing. So I cooked.

Fannie Farmer was my secret social weapon, along with another beat-up old book I still have, titled *Cooking for Company*. I love the way that sounds. I also love what happens when you do cook for company.

If it's not something you do much or at all, give it a try. These recipes are simple. The point of cooking for company is to do it. It's more about the company than the food. These days, people tend to be extremely grateful for a meal or snack that someone prepared just for them.

POPCORN OF THE GODS

When what you want is popcorn, the force is strong. When you make it this way, you have arrived at popcorn perfection. Have a few nuts and some raw veggies along with it, and it's a meal. If you're feeding kids, this is always a smash hit. At the pro level, you'll teach those kids to make it themselves, and serve it with a side of sliced apples dipped in nut butter.

For this, flames are best. A gas stove with a good strong "high" setting, or a glass grill, or an open fire with a grill on top. Use a lightweight kettle with a good fitting lid: glass if possible, that lets you see exactly what the kernels are doing.

directions Melt half vegan butter and half oil in the bottom of the pan: enough so it's about 1/4 inch deep, covering the whole bottom at that depth. Put enough popping corn in to mostly cover the bottom of the pan, one kernel deep. Put the lid on, and move it gently over a high flame until the kernels start to pop; keep shaking the pan until the popped kernels fill it up.

Pour the hot popcorn into a serving bowl, and sprinkle generously with truffle salt and nutritional yeast flakes.

ingredients

Popping corn

Coconut oil

Vegan butter

Truffle salt

Nutritional yeast flakes (or powder)

1 oz. 3.5 cup serving:

Calories 120

Total fat 1 g

Sodium 2 mg (plus truffle salt)

Total carbs 21 g

Fiber 3.6 g

Net carbs 16.4 g

Protein 3 g

1 Tbsp. vegan butter:

Calories 90

Total fat 10 g

Saturated fat 8 g

Sodium 65 m

1 Tbsp coconut oil:

Calories 117

Total fat 14 g

Saturated fat 12 g

Sodium 65

BLISTERED PADRON PEPPERS

No, they're not hot. No, not scary. Gorgeous green, slightly spicy; every once in a while you get one that's almost hot, but never fear.

· The hard part may be finding them fresh. Their season is mid-to-late summer, and you'll find them at farmer's markets, health food stores, and produce markets.

directions Wash the peppers, cut off most of the stem or pull the stems out completely, if you prefer. Heat up cast iron skillet with just a smidge of your favorite olive oil. Dump the peppers in, and let them get singed—"blistered"—on all sides, which should only take a few minutes. Sprinkle with your favorite smoky salt. Done.

Got some left over? Doesn't happen at my house, but, hey. If it did: chop roughly and throw into pasta, a casserole, eggs, or beans. Or freeze 'em. Great to be able to pull a few, frozen, out of a bag and toss them into something.

12 Peppers:
Calories 23
Total fat 2 g
Saturated fat 0 g
Sodium 194 mg
Potassium 0 g
Total carbs 1 g
Fiber 1 g
Net carbs 0 g
Protein 1 g

ingredients

Fresh padron peppers

Olive oil

Smoky salt

EMERGENCY SMOKED SALMON

Nothing better to pull out for a lazy dinner on a summer night, or in front of the fire in chillier weather. Couple of pals show up and it runs into lunchtime? Here ya go. By now, you've figured out the beauty of always having something you can pull out and make into a meal, or a mini-meal, whether you're just treating yourself or a pal or two. Here's a super easy, fast one that looks great, and always tastes perfect.

Please note that the first ingredient, salmon, is "wild-caught" salmon. Why does it matter where the salmon is from? Farmed salmon is less expensive, but full of antibiotics and other stuff you don't want in your body. Don't believe me? Look it up. Then buy wild-caught. Toldja. By the time this recipe is in print, you may be able to find "responsibly raised" salmon, in which case, buy it. Just know, always, exactly what you're putting in that fabulous body of yours. It's the only one you've got.

directions Peel and slice the cucumbers. Finely chop the red onion. Toast the bread. Put a glop of vegan cream cheese on each slice of toast. Squish a few capers on top of the cream cheese. Cut the smoked salmon into bite-size pieces, and put some on each piece of toast; top with chopped red onion and a squeeze of lemon. Dinner is served. Or, even easier, make a pretty platter with all of it and let everybody make their own.

ingredients

Smoked wild-caught salmon

1 or 2 cucumbers

Lemon

Vegan cream cheese

Capers

Red onion

Good sourdough bread or whole grain crackers

Creamy Hot Artichoke Dip.
1 can (14 oz) Artichokes hearts drain
& chop.
1 cup Best Food mayo.
1 cup grated Parmesan Cheese
1 clove of garlic finely chopped
Combine all Ingredients &
bake uncovered at 350°
25 min. or until heated thru

AUNT FROSTIE'S HOT ARTICHOKE DIP

Before she was Aunt Frostie, she was Mildred Wise, of Ada, Oklahoma, with a streak of white hair right in the front of her redder-than-red hair, hence the name Frostie. Of those days in Oklahoma, growing up in the midst of the Great Depression, she liked to tell me that unlike many, she "never went hungry. Never. We always had a garden, with enough to share."

She met my Uncle Roscoe, my mother's brother, during World War II in New York City, where she'd gone like so many others to find a way to help. It was a blind date, by her accounting, and Uncle Rocky, a cocky army cavalryman and firefighter, Californian through and through, opened the conversation with "So that's what an Okie sounds like!"

She always claimed she married him for spite.

Some of my best childhood memories are of summers with Aunt Frostie and Uncle Rocky in Morgan Hill, California. There was always the great smell of something cooking, fresh from her garden, or from the cherry and apricot orchards surrounding their place.

Thanks to my friend Cotton, this perfect old recipe, in Aunt Frostie's handwriting, became part of the kitchen island when she painted it for me, for which I'll be forever grateful.

Now you have it too, plus my vegan updates.

In the '50s and '60s, this dip was served at who-knows-how-many suppers and gatherings, at a time when tables were laid carefully, maybe even competitively, for friends every week or so.

Serve it with some amazing bread or good chips, like Corn Dippers from Trader Joe's.

directions Combine all ingredients and bake, uncovered, at 350° for 25 minutes or until heated through.

Whole recipe:
Calories 1860
Total fat 144 g
Saturated fat 8 g
Sodium 1450 mg
Total Carbs 48 g
Fiber 28 g
Net carbs 20 g
Protein 50 g

ingredients

1 14-oz. can artichoke hearts, chopped

1 cup Vegenaise

1 cup grated or shaved vegan parmesan or nutritional yeast flakes

1 clove garlic, finely chopped

The name of the Paint pony Aunt Frostie was riding in this photo has been lost to history, but her stories and her recipes are still a big part of my kitchen. Aunt Frostie would have been about 19 when this photo was taken, toward the end of the 1930s.

Set the table.

Setting the table isn't just setting the table. It's a magical act. When you set places for people, you make a space for good things to happen. When you set a table well, you also make it beautiful, or fun, or inspiring. In fact, you can make the table so nice that people will already think things taste good before they even sit down.

People want to feel like they're welcome, and they belong. When they see a place all set for them, they know you're happy to have them at the table. What's better than that?

Cloth napkins make a table look like you mean business about your food, your company, and your time at the table. They feel good in your hand and on your lap, which is where they should spend the meal. They're very handy when you get some goo on your hand or your shirt during the meal. In France, each person puts their cloth napkin back in a bowl or basket with a special fold or knot so they know it's theirs at the next meal. In the West, we pretty much throw 'em in the laundry after a meal, unless they're barely used. But that's better than throwing them away like a paper napkin, right?

GUACAMOLE

One more way to eat avocados. Because, in addition to being delicious in so many ways, they are nutrition-packed superfoods. The fats in avocados are good for your heart and your arteries, not to mention your skin and hair. Tons of vitamins and minerals. Plus, they're packaged so brilliantly in their own gorgeous dark green skin, which will go right into the compost. No plastic. No refrigeration necessary. They just sit on the countertop, in a nice little bowl or basket, looking great, waiting to wow you.

Everybody makes guacamole their own way, or buys their favorite ready-made and swears by it. I've never found one as simple or as good as this.

directions Put everything in a bowl and squish it up as chunky or as smooth as you like. No, really. That's it.

ingredients

1 avocado

Juice of 1/2 lime

1/3 cup or more of good salsa verde

Salt—smoky is great

1 cup:

Calories 250

Total fat 21 g

Saturated fat 3.1 g

Sodium 374 mg

Potassium 804 g

Total Carbs 15 g

Fiber 11 g

Net carbs 4 g

Protein 3 g

VEGAN CEVICHE

You could make it with actual fish, if you had the right kind of fish, fresh off the boat. But since the chances of that are slim, how about this cool fish-free version that's just as great?

directions Bring salted water to a boil in a large pot on high heat.

Fill a large bowl with ice and water. Drop cauliflower into the boiling water and cook for 2 to 4 minutes. (If you're fresh out of cauliflower, use 2 cans of hearts of palm, drained and chopped, uncooked, right out of the can.)

Drain the cauliflower, cool it in ice water for a few minutes, then chop it into small pieces.

In a large (pretty!) bowl, combine the cauliflower, tomato, green onion, cilantro, jalapeño, avocados, lemon and lime juices, salt, pepper, olive oil and mix well. Then wipe the edges, to make it Instagrammable. Serve it with tostadas, or corn tortilla chips, lemon slices, and Tapatío. Refrigerate it for an hour or so if you can. If the situation is more urgent, just dive in.

And what, you're wondering, is Tapatío? Thank you for asking! It's hot sauce. But not too hot. The brand name Tapatío comes from the particular company in Vernon, California, where the sauce is produced. "Tapatío" is the name given to people from Guadalajara, Jalisco, where the company's founders emigrated from.

1/4 recipe:

Calories 260

Total Fat 21

Saturated fat 3 g

Sodium 245 mg

Potassium 655 g

Total carbs 18 g

Fiber 7.5 g

Net Carbs 10.5 g

Protein 5 g

ingredients

2 heads of cauliflower

1 cilantro bunch chopped

1 jalapeño chopped (remove seeds and veins)

1 bunch green onions sliced

4 Roma tomatoes chopped

2 avocados diced

1 cup lime juice

1 cup lemon juice

1 tsp. salt plus more for boiling water

1/2 tsp. pepper

2 Tbsp. olive oil

It's never just about the food.

Food isn't just food. It's the part of the meal you eat, but it's not the only part that nourishes you.

There is magic in candles, for example, which I buy in bulk online, partly because we live in the country where the power can go out any time, and partly because nothing makes you look better, or your food taste better, than a few candles. Got a couple of pals coming over? Watch their faces light up, literally, when they see you've put candles on the table in their honor. Make sure the candles are unscented, though. You don't want anything conflicting with the wonderful aromas coming from your kitchen.

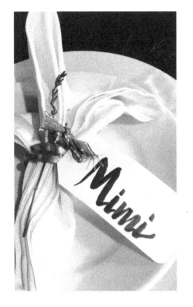

Keep the lighting low and friendly, always, and put some tunes on if it seems right. Ella Fitzgerald, The Stones, Robert Cray, Chopin. Whatever you love. And when you make a pot of Genius Soup or beans, text somebody cool and ask them over. When they want to know what they can bring, tell them flowers or wine or their favorite coffee beans: make sure they know you don't eat sugar. They'll be so grateful for a home-cooked meal, it won't matter. And if they bring up the whole "golly, how do you live without pastry!" thing, pull out those Badass Brownies. Badaboom.

PASTA VERDE

Dark greens are easy to grow yourself and very inexpensive to buy, which is kind of crazy, because if they charged you according to how good they are for you, this dish would cost zillions. But don't make it because it will help stave off macular degeneration, or because of all the antioxidants in it. Make it because it's extremely fragrant and delicious and everyone will think you're a genius in the kitchen.

directions Start the water boiling for the pasta, and throw some kosher salt in the pot after it's boiling. Put the pasta into the boiling water, turn the heat off when it returns to a boil, and put the lid on. Follow package directions for doneness as if it were boiling. Chop all the greens pretty fine, so pieces are something like ½" and throw them into the big serving bowl. Don't be aggressive about it unless that makes you happy. Just whack it all up into small pieces and throw it into the big bowl you will serve the finished dish in.

Chop the garlic very fine and throw it on top of the greens. Sprinkle the olive oil and lemon juice over the greens and garlic, then salt and pepper. When the pasta is cooked, scoop some of the hot water out in one of your glass measuring cups—maybe ¾ cup. Drain the pasta, then throw it on top of the greens as fast as you can, along with the hot water you reserved, so the hot pasta and water wilt the greens.

Toss everything together. Put some vegan parmesan cheese and/or more nutritional yeast flakes on it if you like, and use truffle salt if you like that. Add more hot water if you want a moister texture.

Dinner's ready.

If you're lucky, you'll have some leftover to eat tomorrow. It reheats beautifully in the microwave, with some water sprinkled over it. Combine it with leftover Simple Salmon, and it's even more spectacular.

1/4 recipe:

Calories 210

Total Fat 2 g

Saturated Fat 0 g

Potassium 82 mg

Total Carbs 44 g

Fiber 1 g

Net carbs 43 g

Protein 4 g

(You'll have to figure out the rest, according to what you put in it)

ingredients

Chard, spinach, kale, arugula: one or all, doesn't matter exactly how much

1 medium-sized garlic clove (in this case, size does matter: too much and you'll have a lonely night)

Green onions if you have 'em

Parsley or basil if you have any, fresh

Brown rice pasta, for however many servings you'll need or the whole bag

Fresh juice of one lemon

Good olive oil: your very best

Salt (truffle salt is great in this), pepper

Cooked or canned beans (limas, cannellinis, white kidney beans)

Nutritional yeast flakes

125

FRENCH-AS-HELL LENTIL CASSOULET

Paris, the '60s. I'd gone over with a one-way ticket on the Bremen, an old German passenger liner, with a couple hundred dollars and the Bordeaux address of a friend, Thierry, from UCLA, in my pocket. The idea was to become a fashion illustrator, but the closest I got was selling newspapers on the street.

Since it was Paris, even the lowliest school or street food was exotic and fabulous to me. I fell hard for the bean dishes that were a staple, usually flavored with lamb, duck, or goose fat and lots of garlic, and have been trying ever since to make my bean pots as wonderful.

By now, hopefully, you've read all about how good beans and legumes are for you, and we'll move right ahead to how easy they are to cook. My faves are lentils: beluga black or french green. There are lots of other colors and varieties. See what you can find where you are, or online; they'll all be lovely in this recipe.

We're not going to do the French duck, lamb, and goose fat, but if you can find some local grass-fed sausage, or vegan sausage, freeze it, and pull it out when you want your kitchen to smell as heavenly as that little place on the Left Bank with the grandma cooking in the back.

directions Cut two or three grass-fed beef or pork or vegan sausage into chunks and sauté in a large saucepan with a little broth from the soup.

Cover the cooked sausage with a couple of quarts of Genius Soup, which you made recently or froze last week. Right? You did, right?

Add a package of washed lentils and simmer, with lid on, until they're tender, using package directions if you have them. Usually a half hour or so.

To doll it up, put the finished mixture in a deep, pretty casserole, and cover the top with chopped whole grain sourdough bread pieces or corn chips and sprinkle vegan parmesan shavings and nutritional yeast flakes on top. Heat it in the oven at about 375° until the top is browning.

Serve with a blop of pesto, from page 105, spooned on top.

So French. So good.

Thierry patiently sat for me at his folks' house in Bordeaux. Happy to say we're still pals, 55 years later.

ingredients

Genius Soup (page 92)

Vegan or grass-fed sausage

Green or black lentils

Bread or chips for topping

Vegan parmesan and/or nutritional yeast flakes

Sketch by the author, Paris, 1966.

SUREFIRE POTLUCK SLAW

This will hold up in the heat, with no worries about the mayo going bad. Light and slightly acidic, not too sweet or creamy. Easy. Fabulous. Vegetarian, vegan. Add some orange-flavored cranberries from Trader Joe's, if you feel like it, or some nuts, and turn it into a complete vegan meal.

directions Slice the veggies, stir the dressing ingredients together and pour them over; toss it together, throw on the seeds. Put some edible flowers on it, like we did, to make it even prettier.

ingredients

Thinly sliced green and purple cabbage; (not chopped, sliced in ribbons), at least 1/2 head each color

2 or 3 shredded carrots

2 or 3 thinly sliced green onions (if you want)

A sprinkle of your favorite seeds (chia, celery, hemp, whatever)

1/4 cup apple cider vinegar (or good balsamic)

1 Tbsp. good, grainy mustard

1 tsp. sweetener (unless your vinegar is sweet)

1/4 cup olive oil

Salt and pepper

1/6 recipe with 1 Tbsp. hemp seed:

Calories 147

Total fat 10 g

Saturated fat 1 g

Sodium 117 mg

Potassium 423 mg

Total carbs 13 g

Fiber 5 g

Net carbs 8 g

Protein 3 g

DEVILED EGGS

Yes, these are better than Aunt Ruth's. Way better. The secret is the truffle salt and the simplicity. And why, you ask, are we talking about deviled eggs in a vegan-ish book for diabetics? Because, dear friends, although they are full of animal fat, they are also full of nutrition, assuming they're from lovely, happy, well-brought-up hens who live nearby. And they're delicious. Not for every day, but superb party food, even if the party is very small.

directions Boil and peel the eggs. Or, wait. Let's back up.

How, exactly, DO you boil an egg?

Put the eggs in a saucepan or pot with enough water to cover them. Bring the water to a boil; sprinkle in some salt. Keep them boiling for three minutes, then turn heat off and let the eggs sit in the hot water until it cools.

Remove the yolks and mix with everything but the paprika, capers, or turmeric. Squish or squeeze the yolk mix into the whites.

Don't even think about adding pickle relish. Just don't.

Put the capers, paprika, or turmeric on top, with a little tiny bit of red pimiento if you want. Make faces!

6 eggs, from happy, well-adjusted chickens from good families

2 Tbsp. Vegenaise Original

1 heaping tsp. Dijon mustard

Truffle salt to taste

Capers

Paprika or turmeric or both

Pimiento (optional)

Two halves with pimientos:

Calories 105

Total fat 8 g

Saturated fat 2 g

Sodium 493 mg

Potassium 110 mg

Total carbs 2 g

Fiber 1 g

Net carbs 1 g

Protein 7 g

RANCH DRESSING

Mix yourself up a batch of this and do all kinds of things. Who doesn't love Ranch Dressing? And here it is, with all of the flavor and none of the dairy. No fresh dill? Go without. Still great. Serve it with sweet potato oven fries, on grilled sandwiches, tostadas, veggie burgers, blistered padrons, grilled veggies...maybe even salad.

directions throw it all in a food processor or blender and whirl until the big chunks are gone. Add a bit more soy milk if you need to.

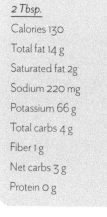

2 Tbsp.
Calories 130
Total fat 14 g
Saturated fat 2g
Sodium 220 mg
Potassium 66 g
Total carbs 4 g
Fiber 1 g
Net carbs 3 g
Protein 0 g

ingredients

8 oz. package of vegan sour cream (or 8 oz. coconut cream mixed with 1 Tbsp. lemon juice; let stand for 1 minute)

1 garlic clove, minced

1/4 tsp. salt

1 cup Vegenaise

2 Tbsp. parsley (fistful)

2 Tbsp. fresh dill (fistful)

1 Tbsp. fresh chives

1 tsp. Worcestershire sauce

1/2 tsp. black pepper

1/2 tsp. vinegar

1/4 tsp. paprika

1/4 to 1/2 cup soy milk (to make it as thick as you want)

BEST-EVER TARTAR SAUCE

Two ingredients. Two. Because you let somebody else make the hard part, which goes under the brand name Vegenaise.

You probably won't need this with the Simple Salmon, page 152, but it's a great way to elevate frozen vegan chicken-like thingies.

directions Put a blop of Vegenaise about the size you think you want in a bowl. Going it alone? Smallish blop. Got pals coming over for supper? Make it a smallish blop times however many pals are on their way.

Blot most of the liquid off a couple of slices of kosher dill pickle, chop it into 1/8" to 1/4" chunks, and mix it with the Vegenaise. If it's game night, you might want to go with a whole pickle.

Boom. Best tartar sauce ever. You don't need to tell anybody how easy it was.

1 Tbsp. Vegenaise Original + 1 spear pickle:

Calories 84

Total fat 9 g

Saturated fat .5 g

Sodium 353 mg

Potassium 2 mg

Total carbs .8 g

Fiber .3 g

Net carbs .5 g

Protein 0

ingredients

Vegenaise

Dill pickle

SUMMER SQUASH CASSEROLE

It's July or August, and you have squash coming out of your eyeballs, right? You don't? You didn't plant those squash plants in June? Well, never mind. Next time. For now, fill your basket at the farmer's market with some zucchini, yellow squash, summer patty-pan squash—doesn't matter what kind. I like the way it looks when you mix them up in a dish, so you get some interesting colors and shapes. This casserole is a great way to use up a lot of it, plus all those half-gone cheeses in the fridge. It looks, smells, and tastes like an old-timey summer supper at Grandma's, if your grandma really knew how to handle a crookneck squash.

directions Slice all the squash up as thin as you can without losing a finger. Sauté squash and onions in olive oil—just a bit—in a large skillet; add salt and pepper. Stir and cook until the squash and onions are fairly soft, but not mushy. Stir together the egg, yogurt, Vegenaise, and hard cheeses totaling about a cup, then add it into the squash mixture. Put it into a large casserole you've greased with olive or coconut oil, top with nutritional yeast flakes then crushed chips; sprinkle vegan cheese generously over the chips and bake for about 20 minutes at 350°.

ingredients

Olive oil

Squash: 4-6 pounds or more, various sizes and types; whatever you've got

1 medium-sized onion (any kind)

Salt, pepper (truffle salt is great)

1/3 cup vegan cream cheese

1/4 cup Vegenaise

1 egg or replacer

Vegan feta, cheddar, jack cheese, shredded

Whole grain or gluten-free chips

Nutritional yeast flakes

1/8 whole recipe:	
Calories	154
Total fat	7 g
Saturated fat	1.25 g
Sodium	169 mg
Potassium	0 g
Total carbs	18 g
Fiber	5 g
Net carbs	13 g
Protein	5 g

Family Supper

Did you notice the progression from "Cooking for Company" to "Family Supper?" There's a reason for that. It's in order of difficulty, based on the crowd. Pleasing company is not so difficult. They're grateful. They're not doing the cooking and hosting.

Pleasing people at a potluck is almost as easy, with the additional challenge of having to leave the food on the table for a few hours.

A lot of the people at the potluck may not be close friends, so they'll be polite, mostly, and more worried about their dish than yours.

(This doesn't apply if you are part of an extremely competitive book club or church group, where "best banana pudding" is a thing, like a perpetual trophy.)

Your family? Not so easy.

Your challenge is to not only heal yourself with food, but to get your family to buy in. Families face at least three huge challenges in this regard.

Challenge One: everybody's going in six different directions every day. Parents either work outside the home or are seriously involved in community or caregiving. Kids are racing from martial arts to piano to Mandarin lessons to scouts to volleyball or soccer, homework and tutoring.

Challenge Two: everybody, starting in elementary school in many cases, has their face in a phone.

Challenge Three: nobody wants to let go of that phone, so the phones wind up at the table. So you need a rule about that. No phones at the table. No eating except at the table. And then you have to be firm and cheerful and consistent to keep the rule sacrosanct.

The pack gathers.   139

When you sit folks around a table and give them something good to eat, magic happens.

If you've grown it and cooked it yourself, the magic is multiplied. But even if you start with putting food you grabbed somewhere on plates, on a table you've set, there's still magic.

Recliners don't count. And, listen, I was right there when the TV Table became a thing. They don't count, either. Beanbag chairs? Nope. The chairs (or cushions, if you're closer to the floor) can be funky and mismatched—all the better, in my book—and the table can be humble. But you have to sit down, hopefully with at least one other person, and look at each other. And talk.

What do heads of state do when they need to communicate something essential to one another and their respective countries? They sit down to a table and share a meal.

When you offer a meal, and a meal is accepted, a peace process has begun. Scale doesn't matter. So, sit down. Eat. Make peace. Even if only for a few minutes.

SMOOTHIES

Lots of folks think of them as breakfast, but what's wrong with a smoothie for dinner, when it's just you and your surly 13-year-old, or when nobody is looking? Go for it.

Smoothies are a painless, completely yummy way to get those dark greens in. Toss them in with the blackberries, and they slide right down. Even, as a pal pointed out recently, when you're pregnant and starving and nothing sounds good.

Plus, a smoothie comes with a special pass to not eat at the table. It's okay, in a pinch, to down one of these genius concoctions as you crank out one more email before you run out the door. Just promise me you'll sit down for at least one meal later in the day.

When you make yours at home instead of grabbing one at Smoothie-O-Rama, it won't have sugar in it unless you add it. And you don't need to. Difference is also in cost: a dollar or so to make your own; five to eight times more if you buy it at Smoothies-R-Us. Plus the aggravation and the wait.

Pro tips

Freeze ripe bananas, cut in half, peeled, so you can drop some in for a freezy, creamy texture.

Add a scoop of protein powder (pea-based for vegans and vegetarians) or some frozen peas or cannellini beans for a more substantial meal.

Keep a bag of frozen blackberries, blueberries, or mixed berries to add for sweetness, color, and to balance bitter greens.

Keep a supply of chopped frozen spinach handy.

A squeeze of lemon or lime takes away any bitterness from greens.

Add a bit of sweetener to any of these: you won't be adding any calories, or fat, or anything but sweetness.

Add more water or soy/coconut/whatever milk any time you need to.

Substitute arugula, spinach, kale, chard for one another any time. It won't change the flavor much, and you'll be getting your greens.

SPINACH SWEETIE

1/2 banana

3/4 cup mixed frozen berries

1/2 tsp. vanilla

1 scoop protein powder (or 1/2 cup peas or beans)

3/4 cup unsweetened soy milk

1 tsp. sweetener

Calories 190
Total fat 1.5 g
Saturated fat 0 g
Sodium 230 mg
Potassium 225 mg
Total carbs 25 g
Fiber 7 g
Net carbs 18 g
Protein 15.5 g

GREEN MONSTER

1/2 cup (or more) soy milk

1 Tbsp. almond butter

1 banana

2 cups mixed greens (kale, chard, spinach, arugula)

With 4 oz. banana:
Calories 256
Total fat 11 g
Saturated fat 1 g
Sodium 136 mg
Potassium 901 mg
Total carbs 34 g
Fiber 6 g
Net carbs 28 g
Protein 8 g

GLOWING GREENS

1 kiwi

1 banana (fresh or frozen)

1/4 cup fresh or unsweetened pineapple

2 celery stalks

2 cups spinach

1 cup water or ice

Calories 194
Total fat 1 g
Saturated fat 0 g
Sodium 124 mg
Potassium 994 mg
Total carbs 47 g
Fiber 8 g
Net carbs 39 g
Protein 3 g

Nutritional value will vary if you use almond, coconut, or another milk.

APPLE/BERRY BEAUTY

1 cup mixed berries (raspberries, strawberries, and blueberries)

1 large apple, cored, peeled

2 cups spinach

1 cup water (or unsweetened almond or soy milk)

PINEAPPLE BANANABOAT

1 cup pineapple

1 banana

1 apple

2 cups spinach

1 cup water

Calories 318
Total fat 1 g
Saturated fat 0 g
Sodium 62 mg
Potassium 1171 mg
Total carbs 81 g
Fiber 12 g
Net carbs 69 g
Protein 4 g

Apple/Berry Beauty Variations

with water instead of almond or soy milk:

Calories 168
Total fat 1 g
Saturated fat 0 g
Sodium 44 mg
Potassium 352 mg
Total carbs 36 g
Fiber 11 g
Net carbs 25 g
Protein 2 g

with unsweetened soy milk:

Calories 248
Total fat 5 g
Saturated fat 1 g
Sodium 104 mg
Potassium 652 mg
Total carbs 40 g
Fiber 12 g
Net carbs 28 g
Protein 2 g

with unsweetened coconut milk:

Calories 213
Total fat 5 g
Saturated fat 4 g
Sodium 64 mg
Potassium 382 mg
Total carbs 37 g
Fiber 11 g
Net carbs 26 g
Protein 3 g

KALE/APPLE GREENIE

2/3 cup almond milk (unsweetened)

3/4 cup ice

1-1/2 cups kale (chopped)

1 stalk celery (chopped)

1/2 red or green apple (cored and chopped)

1 Tbsp. ground flax seed

1 tsp. sweetener

Calories 154

Total fat 6 g

Saturated fat 0 g

Sodium 129 mg

Potassium 653 mg

Total carbs 12 g

Fiber 6 g

Net carbs 6 g

Protein 7 g

KALE/STRAWBERRY/ BANANARAMA

(Serves 2)

1 frozen banana

1 cup unsweetened soy milk

1 cup strawberries (fresh or frozen)

1 cup kale (chopped)

1/2 tsp. vanilla

1/2 cup water or ice

Whole recipe:

Calories 268

Total fat 5 g

Saturated fat 1 g

Sodium 103 mg

Potassium 1271 mg

Total carbs 48 g

Fiber 9 g

Net carbs 39 g

Protein 12 g

MIMI'S MAC'N'CHEESE

From the radioactive orange goo in the familiar little box to the mushy stuff offered as a side in "down home" restaurants, even the worst of it is comforting and yummy, in its humble, bland way.

So imagine, if you will, mac'n'cheese elevated to truly fabulous, both in taste and nutrition. Just remember, you must never tell your guests (or your grandkids, or son-in-law) that what you're serving is healthful in any way. Buzzkill. Let them get a whiff of it coming out of the oven, give them a small serving with a little side-eye, and enjoy the bait-and-switch.

Feel-good bonus: read the chip label to be sure they're gluten-free, and then the entire dish is gluten-free.

directions Preheat the oven to 375°. Cook the macaroni: dump it into boiling, salted water, return the water to a boil, cover the pot, turn the heat off, and let it sit for about 10 minutes. Test for doneness the same way you would for boiling pasta, then get it out of there before it's mushy. Rinse and drain.

Grease a casserole—something in the neighborhood of 9 x 13" or 10 x 10"—with coconut oil.

Make Cauliflower Soup/Sauce per instructions on page 98, and mix in Dijon mustard.

Put a layer of macaroni in the casserole dish, then a layer of cauliflower soup + mustard, salt, pepper, then a layer of shredded vegan cheese blend. Repeat with macaroni, soup, then vegan cheese. Top with a covering of crushed chips and cover chips with shaved vegan parmesan, or vegan provolone, and nutritional yeast flakes. Bake until bubbly and cheese has browned a bit on top.

1/8 whole recipe:

Calories 372

Total fat 10.5 g

Saturated fat 2.3 g

Sodium 255 mg

Potassium 257 g

Total carbs 60 g

Fiber 4 g

Net carbs 56 g

Protein 10 g

ingredients

1 package brown rice macaroni or "penne pasta"

1 head raw cauliflower

1 cup broth or unsweetened coconut (or soy) milk, or a mix

8 oz. vegan feta cheese

8 oz. vegan cheddar, shredded

4 oz. vegan shredded cheese blend—mozzarella, provolone, parmesan, etc.

Black pepper or lemon pepper

Truffle salt—at least 1/2 tsp

1/2 teaspoon Dijon mustard, or more

Good quality multigrain tortilla chips or corn chips (read the label!)

Nutritional yeast flakes

SIMPLE SLAW

What we all need, diabetic or not, is food that waits for us, patiently, in the fridge, for that moment when we come roaring in the front door or down the stairs and need food right now. Not a meal, necessarily, but food that tastes good, feels good to chew on, and is not gonna spike your blood glucose.

This dish is deceptively simple, as are so many good things. You make yourself a batch, and it keeps for a week, well-covered. It's the perfect instant side dish for vegan chicken tenders or salmon. It's great on a hot or cold sandwich. You can throw some cashews in it and make it a whole meal. A lot of kids like it. It's familiar and comforting, crunchy and delicious. It's cheap. It has virtually no carbs. Every tablespoon of Vegenaise is from 90 to 110 calories of fat, so there are calories, but it doesn't even register on the carb scale. And it's almost entirely made of cabbage: a leafy, cruciferous vegetable, plus gorgeous peppers and carrots full of vitamin C and A.

directions Chop the vegetables, finely. A head of cabbage makes a fair amount of slaw; add enough carrots and peppers for color. If you don't have the cranberries, no worries, but...if you do...mmmmmmm. Yes, those orange-flavored cranberries have a bit of sugar added, so take it easy.

> **1 Tbsp. Vegenaise:**
>
> Calories 80
>
> Total fat 9 g
>
> Saturated fat .5 g
>
> Sodium 70 mg
>
> Total carbs 0
>
> Protein 0

ingredients

Cabbage, red or purple, curly or whatever

Carrots if you have 'em

Red, orange, or yellow pepper if you have it (sliced or chopped fine)

Enough Vegenaise to moisten the mixture; 2-4 Tbsp. or more or less

Salt

Pepper

Optional: Trader Joe's Orange Flavored Dried Cranberries, cashews

TOSTADAS

Do you really need a recipe for tostadas? Maybe not. But we're putting one here so you don't forget how easy, how yummy, how kid-friendly, and how nutritious they are. They can also look swell, with all that color and texture on a plate. Okay, so that's great tasting, beautiful, and, hello, another big plus: they're not expensive.

directions If you're using whole beans, blend the beans just until squished, but still chunky, in a food processor or blender. Put some salsa, and smoky salt in the beans as you process.

Heat squished/refried beans in a microwave or a saucepan.

Blister peppers in 1 tsp. olive oil, in an iron pan, hot oven or stove top.

Toast one tortilla per person in a toaster or a 400° oven. Stack each tortilla with beans, shredded cabbage, chopped, blistered peppers, chopped tomatoes, shredded vegan cheese, avocados or guacamole, salsa, then top with chopped fresh cilantro.

1/6 whole recipe:

Calories 275

Total fat 8 g

Saturated fat 2 g

Sodium 481 mg

Potassium 127 mg

Total carbs 39 g

Fiber 10 g

Net carbs 29 g

Protein 9 g

ingredients

serves 4-6 people

Fresh corn tortillas

1 16 oz. can refried or whole beans: pinto, kidney, black, white...whatever you've got

Guacamole (page 80) or avocado slices

Nutritional yeast flakes

Shredded vegan cheese

Padron or jalapeno peppers, blistered in olive oil (page 112)

Good fresh tomatoes

Cabbage, purple and green, sliced very thin

Salsa

Smoky salt (optional)

Fresh cilantro, roughly chopped

TAHINI SALAD

My go-to, everyday favorite salad. Fast, easy, yummy: all the bases covered. Leaves. Seeds. Vinegar. Boom. The secret is in a really good vinegar. My faves are a Gravenstein apple and a Blenheim apricot vinegar from a small local chain of produce markets. Having a couple of fabulous vinegars in your pantry is a great idea for all kinds of reasons, but this recipe is one of the best. Want to turn it into a heartier main course? Top with vegan "chicken" strips or "tenders," cooked according to directions. Or leftover salmon. Or vegan "bacon," cooked crisp. Or some strawberries, sliced, with some walnut pieces. Or...? What's in the fridge?

directions Mix tahini, water, vinegar, salt, and pepper in the bottom of a salad bowl until smooth. Add greens. Toss. Yes, it really is that easy.

1 cup:
Calories 250
Total fat 21 g
Saturated fat 3.1 g
Sodium 374 mg
Potassium 804 g
Total carbs 15 g
Fiber 11 g
Net carbs 4 g
Protein 3 g

ingredients

1/4 to 1/3 cup tahini

Water—same amount as tahini

2 tsp. good vinegar

Lots of your favorite greens: arugula, romaine, butter lettuce, kale...

Salt

Pepper

COWGIRL CAVIAR

Because an avocado a day is good. It's a beautiful appetizer or side dish or a complete meal. It's all right there in that bowl except leaves—unless you want to count cilantro as leaves—so serve it on a pretty bed of arugula or two or three cabbage leaves, or very thinly sliced cabbage. It's a favorite with kids who usually don't like "mixed up" things, because the chunks are recognizable, and because the mangos make it all wonderful.

If you're not crazy about mangos, or can't find them, use a sweet melon instead. Plus, never underestimate the power of marketing: you have to at least taste something called Cowgirl Caviar, right? Or at your house, call it Outlaw Caviar, Deep Dish Desperado, or whatever will work.

directions Chop everything into a bowl, add oil and lemon juice, salt and pepper, toss. Refrigerate until you're ready to serve.

Whole recipe, with 2 mangos

Calories 331

Total fat 14 g

Saturated fat 2 g

Sodium 362 mg

Potassium 722 mg

Total carbs 46 g

Fiber 12 g

Net carbs 32 g

Protein 8 g

ingredients

1 bunch of cilantro

1 jalapeño seeded and diced

1 can black beans (drained)

1 can corn (drained)

1/2 cup diced red onion

2-3 mangos diced

2 Roma tomatoes

1 red bell pepper

1 orange bell pepper

2 medium-sized avocados

2-3 Tbsp. olive oil

Lots of lemon juice!

Salt

Pepper

SIMPLE SALMON

So good it can curl your perfectly blown-out hair. Fresh, wild-caught salmon isn't cheap, but it's a treat, and super nutritious. Give the skin, which separates easily as you eat the cooked salmon, to your fur babies.

directions Wrap the salmon in parchment paper, foil, or place in tight fitting casserole with lid, skin side down. Pour 1/4 cup soy sauce over the fish. Squeeze a lemon over it, (through a strainer—no seeds!) and put a couple slices on top before you wrap it or put the lid on. Bake at 400° for 10-12 minutes, until you hear it sizzling. Pull it out and let it sit for 5 minutes until you unwrap it to serve. You want it to be just barely cooked enough to call it cooked, but not overdone. Serve it with Surefire Potluck Coleslaw, page 128, Simple Slaw, page 147, or on a bed of chopped arugula, or on top of Creamed Spinach, or Cauliflower Soup, made as thick as mashed potatoes.

Got some left over the next day? Toss it with brown rice fettuccine, some chopped greens, and/or coleslaw. Just put the cold stuff in a bowl, throw the hot fettuccine over it, and toss. Add a little warm vegetable broth if you feel like it.

Half salmon fillet (198 g):

Calories 412

Total fat 27 g

Saturated fat 6 g

Sodium 117 mg

Potassium 719 mg

Total carbs 0 g

Fiber 0 g

Protein 40 g

ingredients

Salmon (wild-caught!)
half-pound filet per person

Lemon

Soy sauce

Smoky salt (optional)

Viggo and Hedy wait patiently for the best part of Simple Salmon.

The Big Finish

If you're diabetic, nobody needs to tell you how important dessert is. The fact that you are reading this book, which begins and ends with brownies and donuts and chocolate, is a good indication.

But who ever said that dessert is a bad thing? It's a great thing! As long as you treat it with the same thoughtfulness as you do anything else you eat, it's great. Make it wonderful. Make it beautiful. Make it simple. With these ideas and recipes, you will also be making it healthful, nourishing, and as satisfying and lovely for your innards as it is for your palate.

FRUIT

A few blackberries or cherries, fresh or thawed, in a pretty dish with a dusting of powdered monk fruit sweetener. A piece or two of sugar-free chocolate. A few fresh fruits, in season, cut up together in a bowl. Perfect. Or, go for the really Big Finish with something you've made from the recipes that follow. Just remember to smile, inscrutably, when your family or guests are puzzled that you, healthy food fan, are serving them a decadent, gorgeous dessert.

OLD DOG FARM
Dried Pears

BAKING BASICS

If baking is new for you, congratulations. We'd like to suggest just a few things to keep in mind.

First, when you're baking, it's best to stick with the recipe just as it's written. I know, that's not what you're used to hearing from me, but when it comes to baking, you need to stay with the program. Measure. Follow the sequence as it's written. Don't make any substitutions, unless you've researched it and you know what you're doing. Baking soda/baking powder, for example. Not the same. If the recipe calls for 1 tsp of baking powder, that's what you do. No more, no less, and nothing different, even if it has "baking" on the label.

If you live someplace like Truckee, California—one of my favorite places on earth—you're going to have to adjust the baking time slightly longer for higher elevation.

Always preheat your oven until it tells you it's ready, or for at least 15 minutes.

Gather up all your ingredients and implements before you start. Nothing worse than getting halfway through putting the dough together and finding out you don't have any vanilla.

Grease the pan first.

Have a space identified and cleared to put that hot thing coming out of the oven. Make sure you have a hot pad handy. A clean one. Take them all out of that drawer right now, throw the shredded ones away, and wash the rest. We'll wait.

Don't forget the music. I like to bake to '70s country, loud, because of the memories, and because it's all about trains, porches, mamas, and grandmamas. Plus, of course, drinking and cheating. Perfect for baking.

Now go. Have fun. Lick the beaters.

Everything tastes better baked in a specially shaped pan.

MIMI'S 18-CARAT CAKE

From an old 1940s recipe, updated so you can eat a big chunk of it with no worries.

directions Sift dry ingredients together; mix well with the sweetener and eggs or replacer, then add everything else. Pour into three 9" round pans that have been greased generously with coconut oil, then bake at 350° for 35 to 40 minutes. Cool thoroughly before you frost.

Frost with whipped coconut cream, page 165, vanilla frosting, or cream cheese frosting, page 72. Or, as you see it here, bake it in a beautifully shaped pan, sift powdered monk fruit over it, and call it a cake. Could also be made as cupcakes, just watch timing. An excellent birthday cake for toddlers.

One piece, 1/12 cake (unfrosted)	
Calories 56	
Total fat .25 g	
Saturated fat 0 g	
Sodium 1.2 mg	
Potassium 130 mg	
Total carbs 14 g	
Fiber 3 g	
Net carbs 11 g	
Protein .5 g	

ingredients

2 cups almond flour

1-1/2 tsp. baking soda

2 tsp. baking powder

1-1/2 tsp. salt

2 tsp. or more cinnamon

1 cup powdered sugar substitute

1-1/2 cups applesauce (home made, no sugar!)

4 eggs or replacer

2 cups finely grated carrots

1/2 cup chopped pecans, walnuts, almonds, or pistachios (optional)

4 oz. finely flaked sugar-free coconut

1 can (8.5 oz.) crushed pineapple with juice (no added sugar)

PERFECT PUMPKIN PIE

When you really need something rich and gooey, but totally legal, that screams HOLIDAY, or when you just need something fabulous, rich and gooey, *today*. Which is why I try to always keep beaters, bowl, and coconut cream chilled, just in case.

crust directions Preheat oven to 350°. Toast nuts and oats on a baking sheet (with edges) until golden and fragrant, 10-15 minutes. Cool.

Mix toasted nuts and oats, sweetener, coconut oil, cinnamon, and salt in a food processor. Pulse until nuts are the size of cracker crumbs. Don't overprocess.

Prep a 9" pie plate with a light coating of coconut oil. Press mixture into the coated pie plate, getting as much up the sides as you can, and not leaving the bottom too thick. Squish the bottom with something like a glass measuring cup to get it flat and even. Press the top edge so it's even, to prevent scorching. *(See "step-by-step" next page.)* Bake crust for 20 or so minutes at 350°. Cool on a wire rack.

filling directions Blend filling ingredients in a blender or food processor until completely smooth, then pour and scrape into cooled crust. Bake for 40 minutes, give or take, at 350°, until filling is firm and not jiggly. Cool, then chill pie for at least 2 or 3 hours. Top with Whipped Coconut Cream, page 165.

One piece, 1/12 pie:

Calories 209

Total fat 17 g

Saturated fat 5.3 g

Sodium 204 mg

Total carbs 10.5 g

Fiber 3.5 g

Net carbs 7 g

Protein 4 g

crust ingredients

1-1/2 cups chopped pecans or walnuts

1 cup rolled oats

2 Tbsp. granulated sweetener

4 Tbsp. coconut oil, partially melted

1/2 tsp. cinnamon

1/2 tsp. salt

filling ingredients

15-oz. can pumpkin puree

8 oz. silken or firm tofu

2/3 cup powdered sweetener

2 eggs or replacement

1 Tbsp. (or more) pumpkin pie spice

1/2 tsp. vanilla

1/4 tsp. sea salt

Making your nut crust

Squish the nut mixture as evenly as you can, trying to get the sides covered and just a bit of crust above the sides. Tamp down the top edge so it's fairly even, to prevent high spots from scorching.

It's done when it's just a bit brown around the top edge.

Not in the mood for pumpkin? (**Hard to imagine!**) Fill it with Lemon Curd, page 176.

WHIPPED COCONUT CREAM

There's some fat in this—actually, it's all fat—but a person has to have something whipped and creamy once in a while. It's perfect anywhere you might have used whipped cream, in those less enlightened days when you were still using dairy and sugar. You'll find a small blop, deployed strategically, goes a long way toward true satisfaction.

directions Chill the bowl and the beaters from your electric hand mixer for at least an hour. Now, the hard part: open the can of (chilled for 9+ hours) coconut cream. Be prepared for it to squirt out all over the kitchen. Drain off the liquid that remains into something with a lid, save that coconut milk, but use it within a couple of days. Great on World's Greatest Granola, page 86.

Empty the solids left in your can of coconut cream into the chilled bowl, and beat it with the hand mixer, with chilled beaters, until it's fluffy. Add 1 Tbsp. sweetener and 1/2 tsp. vanilla, mix, then taste. Need a bit more sweetener? Add tsp. or two and mix again.

Keep the whipped mixture in the fridge, covered, until you're ready to use it. Sealed well, it will keep for a week. If you've somehow managed not to eat the whole bowl in a week, freeze the rest.

ingredients

1 13.5 or 14-oz. can full-fat coconut cream, chilled at least 9-10 hours

1 Tbsp. sweetener (to taste)

1/2 tsp. vanilla

Whole recipe:

Calories 1,040 (86 per serving)

Total fat 117 g

Saturated fat 117 g

Potassium 1,040 mg

Carbs 0 g

Fiber 0 g

Net carbs 0 g

Protein 0 g

PEANUT BUTTER COOKIES

This is a recipe you can have in your head, totally memorized, to make on semi-automatic whenever you feel like it. There are only four ingredients, five if you add molasses. They mix up in 3 minutes, bake in 12 to 14. And since all they have in them is peanut butter, egg or egg substitute, baking soda, and sweetener, plus a spoonful of molasses, they are actually GOOD for you. A good source of protein. They smell great coming out of the oven, too. The texture is slightly lighter than old-fashioned peanut butter cookies. Just, please, don't make the mistake of mentioning to anyone that they don't contain sugar or flour. You know how people are. They figure that if it's not full of sugar, refined flour and drowning in butter, it can't possibly be any good.

directions Mix the baking soda with sweetener first, and the rest of the ingredients in no particular order.

When you spoon them onto the baking sheet, squish them down with a fork to make a crisscross on top, the universal symbol for "Watch out, nut allergy people!" The crisscrosses also make excellent crannies for a top sprinkling of powdered sweetener, making it look like you've been baking all day.

Bake them at 350° for about 12 minutes, maybe a bit more, until they're firm, but not too brown.

ingredients

1 cup salted peanut butter. Smooth or crunchy; nothing but peanuts and salt

1 cup "golden" or "brown sugar flavor" sweetener

1 egg or replacer

1 tsp. baking soda

1 tsp. molasses, if you have it, for the "brown sugar" taste

1/12 whole recipe:

Calories 138

Total fat 11 g

Saturated fat 1 g

Sodium 147 g

Potassium 0 g

Total carbs 5 g

Fiber 1 g

Net carbs 4 g

Protein 4 g

UNSUGAR COOKIES

Sugar-free, gluten-free, super easy, and they taste like the sugar cookies my mom and Aunt Frostie made at Christmas.

directions Preheat oven to 350°. Melt the oil or vegan butter just until liquid if it isn't already liquid. Mix with sweetener, vanilla, salt, and water until blended. Add almond flour and baking soda, stir until well mixed. Form into 1" diameter balls, then squish slightly onto cookie sheet prepared with parchment paper or coconut oil. Bake 10-12 minutes at 350° until just barely browning.

Let them cool before you try to move them: they'll flake apart when still hot.

Variations: put a little raspberry or apricot preserves in an indentation on top. Or to stay strictly sugar-free, put a chunk of Trader Joe's Simply Lite sugar-free dark chocolate bar on top of each one before baking. This recipe only makes about a dozen cookies, so double it if there's another human in the house.

ingredients

1/4 cup melted coconut oil or vegan butter

1/2 cup granulated sweetener

1 tsp. vanilla

1/4 tsp. good salt (pink Himalayan or sea salt)

2 Tbsp. water

1 cup blanched almond flour

1/2 tsp. baking powder

Whole recipe: (coconut oil)	Whole recipe: (vegan butter)
Calories 96	Calories 85
Total fat 9 g	Total fat 7 g
Saturated fat 4 g	Saturated fat 1 g
Sodium 356 mg	Sodium 596 mg
Potassium 60 mg	Potassium 60 mg
Total carbs 2 g	Total carbs 2 g
Fiber 1 g	Fiber 1 g
Net carbs 1 g	Net carbs 1 g
Protein 2 g	Protein 2 g

VANILLA SHORTCAKE

Sometimes, what you really, really want is plain vanilla. Good plain vanilla. This recipe makes 12 cupcakes or one cake layer; double it for two layers. It's extremely moist, so kinda tricky for stacking in two layers, but great for cupcakes.

directions Mix dry ingredients together, then mix wet ingredients together til fluffy and add dry ingredients. Bake in a preheated oven at 350° for 20 minutes: if a toothpick comes out clean, they're done. The top will be springy, but not brown. It's yellow cake, after all. Not brown cake.

Cut the cupcakes in half and layer with whipped coconut cream, (page 165) stewed apricots, fresh berries, or lemon curd (page 176).

One cupcake:

Calories 103

Total fat 6 g

Saturated fat 2 g

Sodium 264 mg

Potassium 27 mg

Total carbs 7 g

Fiber 4 g

Net carbs 3 g

Protein 3 g

ingredients

1-1/4 cup coconut flour

1/2 tsp. salt

1/2 tsp. baking soda

1-1/2 tsp. baking powder

1 cup powdered or "baking" grind sweetener

1 egg or replacer

1/3 cup Vegenaise

1/2 cup unsweetened coconut milk

1 tsp. vanilla extract

During June, July, and August, in my part of the country, blackberries are everywhere, sweet and earthy and lovely as blue-black pearls. Wild blackberries and their more domesticated cousins, olallieberries and boysenberries, are full of vitamins C, A, K, antioxidants, and fiber, and some protein. They're already bite-sized and beautiful. No peeling, slicing, or dicing required. Keep a bag or two in the freezer, and you've got the makings of a great smoothie, dessert, or breakfast plate, any time.

Picking your own is always a great reminder:

When things don't appear abundant, change your perspective.

All the bounty of the earth is there, in front of you, if you just try looking from a slightly different angle. Those berries are right under the leaves. You may have to stoop a bit, or move to the right, but then you'll see how many there are, ripe and ready to eat, there for the taking. And yes, there are thorns. Always expect thorns.

The best food you can eat grows wild.

PEAR UPSIDE DOWN CAKE

This is a favorite at Old Dog Farm, because we have two old-timey pear trees of some forgotten variety that were grown not just to survive shipping, but to be eaten, and to taste like heaven. They're not tough enough to survive a crate or a truck, though, and they all ripen in the same couple of weeks, so you have to dry 'em, can 'em, eat 'em, or lose 'em. This recipe will still be good with ordinary pears, like Bartletts, but if you can find really, really good pears, (or grow some!) this is a great way to enjoy them. Serve this with a little Whipped Coconut Cream (page 165) on top.

You'll need teeny loaf pans.

directions Slice and sauté pears with lemon and spice until tender. Grease pans with coconut oil. Smash half the cooked pears and mix with other ingredients. Put the rest of the pear slices on the bottom of the pans, then add batter. Bake at 350° until toothpick comes out clean.

1/3 whole recipe:

Calories 661

Total fat 36 g

Saturated fat 4 g

Sodium 194 mg

Potassium 723 mg

Total carbs 72 g

Fiber 18 g

Net carbs 54 g

Protein 15 g

ingredients

2 eggs or replacer

12 oz. almond butter

1 Tbsp. pumpkin pie spice

1 tsp. baking soda

1/2 cup sweetener

1 tsp. vanilla

Whole lemon

Lots of pears (let's say from 10 large to 14 small)

1/2 cup coconut flour (optional)

Pinch salt

LEMON CURD

Lemon curd is traditionally made with tons of sugar and egg yolks, but we've recreated it with all the lemon fabulousness and none of the sugar or eggs. Why? Because lemon curd is one of those things that our grandmas loved, and we love, too. It's easy, it's a great way to use up those lemons, if you have them in abundance, and it can be pie or sauce or filling or just eaten right out of the bowl at 11 pm, even though you've been advised not to eat that late. If you're going to do it anyway, eat this lemon curd, and don't feel one bit bad about it.

directions In a saucepan, whisk monk fruit and glucomannan, add the rest of the ingredients and turn heat on to medium. Whisk continuously for about 2-3 minutes or until it thickens.

ingredients

1/2 cup monk fruit

1 Tbsp. glucomannan

1/2 cup almond milk

1/4 cup fresh lemon juice

2 tsp. lemon zest

1/8 tsp. turmeric

Whole recipe:

Calories 76

Total fat 1 g

Saturated fat 0 g

Sodium 90 mg

Potassium 92 mg

Total carbs 31 g

Fiber 31 g

Net carbs 0 g

Protein 1 g

BERRY BERRY GOOD GELATO

In the middle of summer especially, you want something icy and creamy after supper. Or, like me, you want it all the time, but you'll settle for after supper. Or sometimes instead of supper. Or before and then after.

directions Throw all the ingredients in a food processor, or mini processor, and process until creamy and blended. Serve immediately.

One serving with soy milk:	*With unsweetened coconut milk:*
Calories 85	Calories 78
Total fat 1 g	Total fat 1 g
Saturated fat 0 g	Saturated fat 0 g
Sodium 12 mg	Sodium 4 mg
Potassium 209 mg	Potassium 175 mg
Total carbs 18 g	Total carbs 17 g
Fiber 5 g	Fiber 5 g
Net carbs 13 g	Net carbs 12 g
Protein 2 g	Protein 1 g

ingredients

(Per person)

One cup frozen mixed berries, blackberries, blueberries, cherries, or raspberries

One blop (2 Tbsp.) or more soy milk (or oat milk or coconut milk)

1/4 tsp. vanilla

1/4 cup powdered sweetener

RHUBARB, THE PINK DESSERT VEGETABLE

Just when you think there will never be another spring, along comes rhubarb, bursting out of the ground with huge, tropical-looking leaves and amazing blossoms that look like they might come up and punch you in the face if you stand there long enough. You cut those blossoms off to encourage growth in the stems, and the stems are what you're going to eat.

Harvesting a big bucket of those gorgeous pink stems in late April is an act of reaffirmation. You've done nothing about it all winter, except to cut the blossoms off in early April or late March. It takes care of itself, appreciates some extra water, and reappears bigger and better every year in the same place from rhizomes beneath the surface. It's free, in other words. It requires no packaging, no carbon products, no transportation. Here at Old Dog Farm, it gets no poisons or sprays, and very little coddling or weeding. It's good food. And, it's a Leafy Green Vegetable, kinda **like celery in drag.**

Is there a downside to rhubarb? Yes. A couple. Eating the leaves will make you sick. Don't eat the leaves. Also, because it is so fibrous, it can have a laxative effect. So if you're going to eat a bucketful, you might want to stay home for a bit.

What if you don't like pink? I can't imagine. But in that case, the green stems of some types are just as edible and fabulous as the pink ones. Rhubarb is also a forgiving ingredient. You can overcook it, fail to measure it, undersweeten it, whatever, and it's just not a problem. Add more sweetener, you're good.

Calories? Negligible. Throw some strawberries in with it, and you've still got negligible calories.

When I harvest a bunch, I cook it down and stick it in the fridge or freezer in mason jars, leaving room at the top.

directions Wash the rhubarb, cut off the cruddy green or brown parts, and cut it into 2-3" long chunks. Put it with a little water in a pan with a lid, and cook it on medium or low heat until it's soft, which will only take 5 minutes or so. Add a spoonful of psyllium if you want, to thicken it, and throw in plenty of your favorite sweetener.

1 cup diced rhubarb:
Calories 26
Fat 0.2 g
Sodium 5 mg
Carbs 5 g
Fiber 2 g
Net carbs 3 g
Protein 1 g

ingredients

Rhubarb, cut into 2-3 inch
chunks

Water

Sweetener, to taste

COCONUT HAYSTACKS

I can't tell you how many chocolate shops I've found with my nose, only to discover cruel disappointment inside. No, they don't have any sugar-free candy. Waaaaah. Sometimes a person just really, really wants good chocolate candy. Here, then, is what to do when you're in need of a fix.

directions If it's just for you, something like 3 squares of chocolate ought to do. For more, adjust accordingly. Melt with the coconut milk in a small saucepan, or nuke it in a dish for just 5-15 seconds. Stir melted chocolate, then add coconut and mix well to coat. Make little stacks on waxed or parchment paper, or a dish, and refrigerate until firm.

Whole recipe:

Calories	64
Total fat	5 g
Saturated fat	5 g
Sodium	0 mg
Potassium	0 mg
Total carbs	2 g
Fiber	2 g
Net carbs	0 g
Protein	1 g

ingredients

1 cup unsweetened coconut (riced or shaved)

3 squares Trader Joe's Simply Lite dark chocolate candy or equivalent

1 Tbsp. coconut or soy milk

Walnuts (optional)

Food is Connection.

Food is how we connect not only with each other, but with the planet. When you pull a tomato or some radishes from the pots on your porch or raised beds in your front yard or community garden, it tastes ten times better than anything wrapped in plastic.

No plastic sticker to try to remove. No plastic wrapper to toss out. No trash. No waste. The part you cut off? Into the compost container, out to the worms, back into the garden. None of this is new to you, but are you doing it? Or are you whining, cellphone in hand, about the failings of your new meal delivery service?

Ranger says "Please, no whining."

Eating thoughtfully benefits way more than you, your brain, your gut, your family, and your social life. By supporting your local regenerative agriculture movement—the farmers who are not just taking from the soil, but building it—you are making a huge contribution to your local community and the earth. Their produce tastes better, is more nutritious, carries no poisons. If you eat meat, choose meat from farmers who are grazing their animals on pastures where they can eat plants that don't make them sick. Corn-fed cattle have to be fed antibiotics to keep them well. Go out of your way, if you have to, to buy eggs, pork, beef, lamb from farmers who care about the health of their dirt, their worms, and all of their critters. By treating their animals better, they're helping keep you healthy, too.

When you buy from a local farmer's market, you're supporting a small, local business. You're buying much better food, with higher nutritional content along with fewer or no pollutants and poisons. You're reducing your carbon footprint, and eliminating plastic packaging. You're buying and eating seasonally, and more likely, simply. All good. Even if sometimes the food may cost a bit more, it's more than a good deal in so many ways. It's *connection*.

Where to shop for food

I can still remember the first time I was ever in a Trader Joe's, in Culver City, CA, in the early '70s. We hipsters had just discovered good sourdough bread, whole grains, coffee beans, curry powder, and some of the other food items that would make our barely-adult lives more wonderful. And boom, here was this little market that had all of them! Not only that, but their prices were great, the folks were nice, and the place had kind of a Southern California fun-in-the-sun feel to it. Sold.

Fast forward 40 or so years later, and the U.S. has caught up with TJ's in terms of appreciating well-made deli foods, "exotic" foods like dried mango, edamame, arugula, and, my favorite, cheap, good bourbon. Trader Joe's prices are still half what the tonier "health food" stores are, and their store-brand stuff is great. Because I've been shopping there for years, and I'm notoriously—shall we say—*frugal*, a lot of the ingredients in this book are from TJ's. For vanilla, boxed broth, pesto, frozen peas and cherries, frozen chicken-like thingies, it's hard to beat.

My second favorite place, second only because it's not always available, is a farmer's market. If you haven't been shopping in a farmer's market, find out if there is one near you, where it is, and try it. Get to know the people growing food near you, and help them help you save the world.

Third favorite, or maybe first favorite, depending on where you live, is signing up for a CSA (Community Service Agriculture) box, either to pick up or be delivered. Some are seasonal, some are year-round. Everything in the box is always good, healthy food, with no wasted packaging. A side benefit is that it will include some produce you're not familiar with, or have never tried, and you will, hopefully, try it. The downside is you will regret all those lost years before you discovered arugula or really good leeks, thanks to your CSA.

Then, there's ordering online. It's a miracle. You press a few keys, and in a day or so, all the monk fruit sweetener or smoky salt you want shows up at your door. Some of the newer services—**Public Goods, Thrive Market**—offer subscriptions and will deliver almost everything you'd buy in a grocery store.

What about chain stores like Ralphs, Raley's, Winn-Dixie, and the rest? I never go in them, because I don't have to. These stores, for the most part, have not been a happy experience for me. At the end of my life, will I wonder why I didn't spend more time wandering the aisles of Krogers? Doubt it.

As of recently, however, most of these chain grocery stores let you phone or email them an order, which they assemble, and which you pick up at their designated pick-up place, which eliminates the whole wandering-the-aisles thing.

What stumps me, though, is how in the world a person is able to navigate those aisles, acres of them, all designed to get you to buy things you probably wouldn't want if you thought a little more about it. Who has the time or energy? I did do an experiment once, a while back, just focused on the cereal aisle. I was looking to see if there was a ready-to-eat cereal that was "healthy" and sugar-free. I read every label on nearly every box. There was, in that whole, long aisle of hundreds of packages, literally nothing even minimally nutritious with no sugar.

If you do choose to wander there, don't let them lead you unto temptation with those displays at the ends of each aisle, full of all the nasty, sugary cakes, cookies, and chips.

Pro takeout tips

There will be times when you need to buy a ready-to-eat meal in a bag. We're all human. We get hungry, and tired, and need to feed other people when there's barely enough of us left to feed ourselves after a day of fighting it out in the trenches somewhere.

When you get it home, or to the office, put away half for the next day. Don't even put it on your plate. Cut it in half, put half on your plate, and put the rest away.

Hold the rice. No white rice, ever. If you order a burrito, for example, with no rice, you'll get extra beans or shrimp or veggies to fill up the space where that rice would have been.

Hold the factory-farmed chicken or beef. Get your burger with a non-meat patty, and ask for vegan cheese. Ask if they have vegan condiments, and order those. Otherwise, put your own—Vegenaise or avocado slices—on at home.

Go for Thai, Vietnamese, or Middle Eastern food. Ethiopian is usually vegetarian and delicious. Japanese? Yes, but hold the rice. Or get brown rice.

Takeout salad is almost always a fine idea, so long as you put your own dressing on it. Make up a batch of Ranch Dressing, page 130, put some in small containers in the fridge, and take one with you when you're out for the day.

When you reheat the second half of your takeout order to eat the next day, add to it, using salsa or avocados or shredded cabbage or red pepper soup to make it more beautiful, bigger, and better.

Here ya go: half of yesterday's takeout shrimp burrito (hold the rice) reheated—nuked—with red pepper soup, purple cabbage. Oh, yeah.

Pro sleeping tips

Are you getting seven, eight, or nine hours of deep, restful sleep every night? Yes? Okay, skip this chapter. If not, please pay attention.

If you're not sleeping, you're not healing. Your body can't do the housekeeping it needs to do unless your systems shut down into deep sleep. You can't get everything you want by just fixing the way you eat and doing a minimum of exercise. You must also fix the way you sleep. Eating, moving, and sleeping are all inextricably connected.

Here's how to sleep like a pro:

1. Turn off or cover every light, including the little tiny red ones on your phone or other electronics, in your bedroom. Pull the shades. Make sure your sleeping room is as dark as you can make it.

2. Don't sleep with your electronics anywhere near you.

3. For at least an hour, or two, before you want to sleep, no electronics. No TV. Reading is fine, and reading on an iPad-type screen is okay, but good old paper books and magazines are best.

4. Set a sensible lights-out time and stay with it, cutting yourself off of your screens an hour or two before.

5. No food for at least four hours before lights-out. More time is better: nothing after 4-5 p.m. Nothing but water or herbal tea.

6. Drink a glass or two of water before bed. Yes, you may have to get up to pee. Peeing is good for you.

7. Use a weighted or very heavy blanket.

8. Make it as quiet as you can. Use earplugs if you need to.

9. If you do wake up, don't stress about it. Turn your clock to the wall and don't look at it.

10. "Dogs in bed can help or hinder, depending on the dog," says Ranger.

Turns out, dear reader, that eating better is not only going to make you happier, but help you sleep, which helps in all kinds of ways, including making all the people around you happier.

Researchers have found that sugar, saturated fat, and processed carbs can disrupt your sleep, while eating more plants, fiber, and foods rich in unsaturated fat—nuts, olive oil, fish, and avocados—helps you sleep. Studies have found that people who don't sleep well have poorer quality diets, with less protein, fewer fruits and vegetables, and a higher intake of sugary and ultra-processed foods. [9] Conversely, in other studies, people who follow a "Mediterranean diet"—nuts, seeds, fish, whole grains, lots of green stuff—sleep longer and better. People who are deprived of sleep have increased appetite, particularly for sugar and carbs, while people who eat more sugar and refined carbs sleep less. In these studies, when people are no longer deprived of sleep, their "normal" appetite returns.

In men, sleep deprivation stimulates increased levels of ghrelin, the so-called hunger hormone, increasing appetite. In women, sleep deprivation leads to lower levels of GLP-1, reducing the signal that makes you stop eating.

What you eat also affects not just the quantity but the quality of your sleep.[10] Studies have found that eating more saturated fat and less fiber from foods like vegetables, fruits, and whole grains led to reductions in slow-wave sleep, which is the deep, restorative kind.

Talking dirt

Let's start with WHY. Why not just throw out all your garbage for the garbage folks to pick up and haul off? You're paying someone to haul your banana peels and coffee grounds a few miles away, process them, pile them up, bury them, or ship them off to some other place, when you could be turning them into the best possible fertilizer for your garden. You don't have a garden? Isn't there a community garden near you? There are also services now who will happily pick up your organic "waste" and take it away to make compost out of it. But if you only have a small patch of dirt, this is a fabulous way to make it productive.

Talk about a no-brainer. It's such an utterly simple thing, and I thought most folks were doing it, but I guess it's a bit like sex that way. Everybody thinks everybody else is doing it way more than they actually are, so nobody talks about it, and everybody thinks there's something just too messy and complicated about it.

NOT.

A little earthy, maybe, but not complicated. Not messy. And everybody should do it.

All you need is a bucket for your sink: a bucket with a handle is good, and some ventilation. Something like this.

Then you'll need a compost bin that goes outside wherever it's convenient, possibly tucked away out of sight, probably not too far from your kitchen. You throw all your vegetable and fruit kitchen scraps into your sink bucket—no animal products, no meat, no dairy, egg whites are fine—then carry it out, whenever it's full or whenever you want, to your outside compost bin and dump it in. You will also put all your yard "waste" into your compost bin: grass clippings, bush clippings, leaves, straw, horse poop (which is entirely vegetable), or cow poop (same). A compost bin has no bottom. It sits directly on the dirt. What happens, then, is that moisture drains out through the bottom, and **WORMS come up from the dirt and process your compost for you.** If

you want extra worms for faster processing, you can buy them. **Or if you have kids, put them to work digging some up and throw them into the bin. The worms, not the kids.**

You'll read all kinds of stuff about the correct ratio of leaves to dirt to scraps to worms, and how often to turn it or water it or whatever, but you really don't have to pay any attention to that. If you're kinda on the anal or OCD end of the scale, you can become a compost nerd and compete with your neighbors for whose compost processes the fastest, or measures the exact right pH, or whose worms appear to be the happiest, perkiest, and best adjusted. Otherwise, just toss (organic—nothing with poisons, no meat) plant materials, including things like paper, into that bin and let the worms, who will find it, appear magically and do all the work.

If you're using one of those services that comes out and sprays unspeakable mystery stuff on your lawn to make a perfect putting green, don't use those clippings. That's poison they're spraying on your lawn, by the way, and you're letting your kids and pets walk on it.

When your compost has finished processing, it will smell lovely and look like the potting soil you buy in bags at the nursery. You will then put it on all your plants, or use it for potting soil, and you will feel so very smug. **Look what you did with your apple peels and old paper napkins!**

Because we now live in an age when it's possible, please think of this book as the beginning of a conversation. Let me know how you're doing with it. Check in on LynneBowman.com for updates, more in-depth discussion about food, and related issues. There's also a list there of video links and book resources, always expanding and being revised.

Plus, take a look at the Lynne Bowman Channel on YouTube, for how-to vids, Q & A, and longer explanations about all kinds of things.

Here are just a few of the good documentaries out there on Netflix and elsewhere about sugar, plant-based eating, and the like, and a great place to start:

Kiss the Ground

The Game Changers

Forks Over Knives

Food Matters

That Sugar Film

Hungry for Change

Fat, Sick and Nearly Dead

Fed Up

Super Size Me

What the Health

In Defense of Food

Food Choices

Vegucated

Food Inc.

The Magic Pill

Revolution Food

Toussaint-Samat

FOO[D]

A HISTOR[Y]

The Jungle Effect

Daphne Miller, M.D.

ON
FOOD
AND
COOKIN[G]

THE
SCIE[NCE]
AND
[L]OR[E] OF
[THE]
[K]ITCHEN

SEL
DU
JARDINIER

Poids Net 500 grammes

Le Père Pelletier
55600 MA[RV]ILLE

Revised
for the
[first] time
[since 19]54 for
tod[ay's] lifestyles

[A] Grateful RECIPES [&c.]

The All New

JOY
of
Cooking

Loren Cordain

The Paleo Diet

TANNAHILL

500 cupcakes *Fergal Connolly*

...bauer,

...ecker

MICHAEL POLLAN   FOOD RULES   AN EATER'S MANUAL

ANDREW WEIL, M.D.

[E]ATING WELL FOR OPTIMUM HEALTH

THE
ESSENTIAL
GUIDE TO
FOOD, DIET,
AND
NUTRITION

PALE[O] *Desserts*   Jane Barthelemy

What to read

Lots of good options here. Please visit LynneBowman.com for a list of links, which is growing all the time, and much more complete. That's also a great place to leave comments, more recommendations, and ask questions.

These are books that are going to change the way you think about food, the way you buy food, and help save the world. We're exaggerating, slightly, because we really, really want you to read these.

David Zinczenko, *Eat This, Not That!* Perfect to carry in the car. Little Brittany is whining for Krispy Kremes? Taco Bell? Just have her read aloud what the damage is for her favorite choices, and then see what Mr. Zinczenko offers as better options.

Michael Pollan, *The Omnivore's Dilemma.* A wonderfully written, readable, elegant, surprising, thoughtful book about where your food comes from. In fact, do yourself a favor and read anything Michael Pollan has written. *The Botany of Desire*, for example, has also been made into a wonderful movie. Or, another swell example:

Michael Pollan, *Food Rules.* It's short, super easy to get through, and makes it all very clear. Carry it with you, along with *Brownies for Breakfast.*

T. Colin Campbell, PhD, and Thomas M. Campbell II, *The China Study.* "...One of the most important books about nutrition ever written—reading it may save your life," according to Dean Ornish, MD, and we concur. It's not just one study, as you might infer from the title, but an overview of lots of nutrition studies that offer very conclusive results

that you've probably never heard about. Campbell explains the reason we don't know about these results is that we've been intentionally kept in the dark. This fact in and of itself is an extremely interesting story. Also good, T. Colin Campbell's *Whole.*

If you can only read one book about food, read this one, and then get all the Michael Pollan books on CD and watch the movie. We can almost guarantee it will change the way you eat, as in "Why didn't I read this years ago?? What have I been doing to myself? My kids?"

Dr. Michael Greger, *How Not to Die.* Dr. Greger is easy to read, thorough, and a great resource for finding the answers to nutrition-related health questions.

Dr. Michael Greger, *How Not to Diet*, offers lots more recipes and research-based information to help you on your plant-based quest.

Mathew Walker, PhD, *Why We Sleep*, is a complete, but highly readable, physiological explanation for how you only heal when you're sleeping.

Bee Wilson, *The Way We Eat Now*, "How the food revolution has transformed our lives, our bodies, and our world."

Source Notes

1   elisabeth.bernstein@wsj.com, "Foods That Help Battle Depression," April 3, 2018, print edition; healthline.com, "Nine Healthy Foods That Lift Your Mood," February 5, 2020.

2   Centers for Disease Control and Prevention, (CDC), 2015.

3   National Diabetes Statistics Report, 2017.

4   CareWire, January, 2016. "According to a study in the Journal of the Royal Society of Medicine, more than half of the patients 'immediately' forgot verbal directions once they left the doctor's office, and half of the information they remembered was incorrect. Hospital patients don't fare much better, with retention rates at the same level and a whole lot more follow-up care information to retain."

5   MayoClinic.org

6   Diabetes.org

7   T. Colin Campbell, PhD, *Whole*, 2014.

8   health.harvard.edu, "Microwave Cooking and Nutrition," February 6, 2019.

9   Anahad O'Connor, "How Foods May Affect Our Sleep," New York Times, December 10, 2020.

10. Ibid

Acknowledgements

Rodger, my partner in everything, thank you. For everything.

Brynja, your time and patience have been invaluable, along with your inspiration.

Kelly, all those miles, walking and talking this book, have kept me going. Literally.

Jake, you made me think it mattered, which made it possible to finish.

Erica, thank you for great, enthusiastic recipe contributions and testing, and so much more.

Jessica, you and your family have helped inspire this effort. Thank you for that, and for help with nutritional stats.

Linda Ravetti and Teri Gwin (and Brynja): so good to have your professional, medical eyes on this. Thank you.

Kevin Lazaruk, you've been a great editor and teacher.

Elise Huffman, you're the best, and Ranger, so are you.

Photographic Sources

Lynne Bowman, almost all of the photos in this book ferpetesake!

Larry Dyer, TOC page 1, 158

Jeff Grubb, page 113

Erica Hernandez, page 121, 130, 150

Elise Huffman, page 23, 123, 153, 154, 177, 183, 185, 186, 188, 189, 192, 201, 198

Jonatan Soares, page 18, 19 and 196,

Art Sources

Thank you, Molly Brown, for her generous permission for use of woodblock art on pages: 64, 87, 93, 94, 104, 151, 183, 195. Go to www.mollybrownart.com to see more.

1. Graphics Fairy, www.graphicsfairy.com

2. Dover Publications, *Food and Drink, A Pictorial Archive from Nineteenth Century Sources*, compiled by Jim Harter, Dover Publications 1983.

3. *The Clip Art Book, A Compilation of More Than 5,000 Illustrations and Designs*, research and introduction by Gerard Quinn, Crescent Books distributed by Crown Publishers, Inc., 225 Park Avenue South, New York 10003, 1990.

4. Adobestock, https://stock.adobe.com/, "AdobeStock_74481778" used on cover.

5. *Pictorial Volume, Handbook of Early Advertising Art, Mainly from American Sources*, by Clarence P. Hornung, 3rd edition, Dover Publications, New York, 1956.

6. *The Cornucopia of Design and Illustration, for Decoupage and Other Arts and Crafts*, Dover Publications 1984.

7. *Harter's Picture Archive for Collage and Illustration, Over 300 19th-Century Cuts*, edited Jim Harter, Dover Publications, Inc., New York, 1978.

8. *Lively Advertising Cut of the Twenties and Thirties, 1,102 Illustrations of Animals, Food and Dining, Children, etc.*, edited by Leslie Cabarga and Marcis McKinnon, Dover Publications, Inc., New York, 1990.

9. *Animals, 1419 Copyright-Free Ilustrations of Mammals, Birds, Fish, Insects, etc., A Pictorial Archive from Nineteenth Century Sources*, compiled by Jim Harter, Dover Publications 1979.

10. Wellcome Library, https://wellcomelibrary.org/, Unless otherwise stated, all content on the site is © The Wellcome Trust and is licensed under Creative Commons Attribution 2.0 UK. This means that you are free to share the content by copying, distributing and transmitting it, but please attribute it to the Wellcome Trust and provide a link to its website https://wellcome.org (opens in a new tab). For any reuse or distribution, you must make these licence terms clear to others. Franz Eugen Köhler, Köhler's Medizinal-Pflanzen - List of Koehler Images. Public domain. File: Cocos nucifera - Köhler's Medizinal-Pflanzen-1897.

11. Wikicommons, https://commons.wikimedia.org/, pages 195 "'Commercial tube compost bin'"; a simple way to hold a compost pile neatly in one place * Taken by Ellen Levy Finch (Elf | Talk) Mar. 16, 2004 * first upload at en.wikipedia by Elf 01:41, 17 Mar 2. Cornelis van Haarlem "A monk and a nun—detail," taken by Vassil on 6 November 2012, public domain, page 40. Dill Pickles Rag.jpg, created: 1 Jan. 1906. Ragtimedorianhenry2010 Johnson—Collection, page 132.

Chicory Root and Leaves, Internet Archive identifier: CAT31284409 https://archive.org/download/CAT31284409/ CAT31284409.pdf "October 30, 1900." Signed, Maurice G. Kains. Division of Botany Circular No. 29. At head of title: United States Department of Agriculture, Division of Botany.

ISBN number: 978-1-7367450-0-7

This book is obviously not meant to replace the care or advice of a medical professional. You should consult your own, vetted medical professional before radically changing your eating habits. Then if you have a problem, especially one that might assume a litigious nature, any blame can be placed on their well-insured, white-coated shoulders, not ours.

Any reference to a brand name product is for information purposes only and is not intended to suggest endorsement or sponsorship by the author of this book.

Book design: Elise Huffman, Santa Cruz, CA, huffmandesign@me.com

About the Author

Lynne Bowman, aka "Mimi," has been featured at women's expos throughout the country, leading retreats and workshops on subjects including grooming for governing, kitchen table culture, power eating, community planning, and the gift of diabetes.

With a lifelong interest in moving people toward healthier, more nourishing ways of living, she teamed up with actress Deidre Hall to write, speak, and teach. Together, they wrote and published *Deidre Hall's Kitchen Closeup* (2010) and *Deidre Hall's How Does She Do It?* (2012).

Lynne's first project as an author/publisher was *Fast, Cheap & Skinny* (1991) with M.K. Streeter.

In 1996, she and her husband fell in love with Pescadero, a little coastal town 35 miles south of San Francisco, and bought an old farm at the edge of the redwoods. As president of the Pescadero Foundation, she has been meddling in a variety of community matters since then, supporting regenerative agriculture, sustainable infrastructure, and working to build affordable homes in rural San Mateo County.

In a previous life, she worked with Silicon Valley companies as a creative director and marketing consultant, winning national creative awards applying consumer strategies to technology products and services.

She was Creative Director at E&J Gallo Winery during Bartles & Jaymes' heyday, and way back before the dawn of time, Advertising Manager at Redken Laboratories, holding various other creative positions with agencies and clients in San Jose, Los Angeles, and on the East Coast. She has also worked as an actress, makeup artist, screenwriter, illustrator, broadcast producer, legal journalist, and television weatherperson.

She is the mother of three grown children, and at this writing, a grandmother of one absolutely perfect grandchild.

lynne@lynnebowman.com
YouTube: Lynne Bowman Channel
Facebook: LynneParmiterBowman

CPSIA information can be obtained
at www.ICGtesting.com
Printed in the USA
LVHW071935110322
713214LV00012B/172

9 781736 745007